Testimony of a Broken Bride

Jesus is the **True** Husband

An Autobiography of
Dr. June Dawn Knight

Published By:

Treehouse Publishers

www.gotreehouse.org

Copyright © 2015 Dr. June Dawn Knight

ISBN-13: 978-1505691023

ISBN-10: 1505691028

CONTENTS

DEDICATION

This book is dedicated to all the Christians who have looked for love in all the wrong places. This is for those who searched for the quest of destiny and found it in our loving savior, Jesus Christ. This is for the broken brides out there!

ACKNOWLEDGMENTS

My Three Beautiful Children!

Brock, Andrew, & Meagan - You children are the rock of my life and thank you so much for the honor to be your mother. God has a plan for our whole family and it will come to pass in Jesus' name!

My children have been through a lot and are the most courageous, smart, beautiful people on the planet. I'm so proud of you kids. I want to thank you for forgiving me and supporting me in my journey with God. We are all on a journey and on a quest to fulfill our destiny.

The greatest lesson of my life story is forgiveness in your hearts. We must all move on and trust God for our tomorrows. It's wonderful that we have Him to put our faith in. A relationship with God is the greatest legacy I could ever leave you children. I pray for you, love you, and believe in you. Without you kids life wouldn't be the same.

Thank you for loving me and standing by me through the thick and thin. I love you always.

My Spiritual Parents

Thank you to my two spiritual sets of parents, Dr. Rod & Joni Parsley and Drs. Christian and Robin Harfouche. Both ministers came from Lester Sumrall and he is from Smith Wigglesworth. Thank you for all the deposits and impartations into my life.

Thank you to all the board members, staff and partners who believe in the vision of We are the Bride Ministries.

Disclaimer:

This book is an autobiography of the life story of June Dawn Knight. Please picture us sitting at a table and I'm reciting to you the memoires of my life. Some memories are very dark but I must tell the story in obedience to God. This book is written according to the recollection of my memories. To my heart before the Throne of God, these memories are the truth. I also want to ensure forgiveness has been given for all involved. God has a plan for every one of us and I pray this book encourages you to never quit and to discover the True Husband for your life.

Reviews

This was a most revealing read openly displaying the pain of this precious woman & her family. Through her complete transparency I could see the struggles and yet the determination to overcome in each season of her life. This book breeds hope and displays the way God can take any of us from pains and mistakes of the past to a future a shining light for all to see His goodness & mercy. He truly does use all things in our lives for divine purposes. While reading the book, you will begin see the Hand of the Lord working throughout even in pain and failures to keep this mighty woman of God turned toward Himself. I felt as though Dr. June was right here in the room with me as the trusted friend that she is. Wonderful.

Dr. Dianna Senkyrik
President, EagleHeart Ministries, Inc.
Bay City, Texas

This book is amazing! I could not put it down. The author brought out things that made me stop and examine my own self. When a book causes you to look deep inside your own self, you know it's good. It also showed in the biography that a person can be brought back to life if only they seek the living water they need to live in Christ. I highly recommend this book. It will open your eyes of how we need to seek our true husband daily.

Wanda Jordan
President, Fresh Oil Ministry, Inc.
Ashland City, Tennessee

I can feel the "genuineness" --- the "purity" of this book.

Dr June has released this book into the Kingdom for such a time as this. This book is a must read for anyone who desires to draw closer to the Bridegroom. He's calling us into a more intimate experience with Him. We must go there!

Pastor John Ortiz
The Gathering Place
Nederland, Texas

Reviews Cont'd

Anyone can relate to "Testimony of a Broken Bride" in the sense that we have all been broken throughout our lives. Dr. Knight has shown how being touched by the love of God can and does transform a person into a new creature as the scripture says. A person cannot be touched by God and stay the same and she has shown how that happens in our lives. For an inspiring story of God's love, hope and transformation you need to read this book.

Penney Major
25 years in ministry
Nashville, TN

1
A BROKEN BRIDE

The Trinity, which is God the Father, God the Son, and God the Holy Ghost, wrote the destiny books for each human before time began. They formed each spirit to be birthed into the Earth for a short amount of time to reveal to mankind another aspect of who God is. Now, this revelation cannot happen unless the human CHOOSES to allow God to finish their life story according to that book. The human can choose to continue in their path of self-absorption and plans or release their life into God's hand, which are unknown futures. Our destiny can go one of two ways: God's way or our way.

How do I know this you ask? This is a revelation that God has granted to me and will be written in full in the next book in this series about the Garden. I will get into more detail at that time. However, for this book's sake, I want you to understand how God wrote my book before time began. The devil probably knows what is coming on the destinies so he tries to thwart the plan from coming forth. After you read this book and realize where God is taking me, you will see all the different ways he tried to take me out and to prevent me from achieving the full destiny that God had for me, along with my family line of prophetic children.

My story is a lot like most people in America in that I was raised in a broken home. I was raised without a father and in an alcoholic home. At five years old the devil molested me, broke up my family and began the patterns of abuse. By the time I was eight years old I wanted to kill myself. At ten years old I discovered a relationship with my creator and at the age of eleven the pastor hurt me greatly which built up years of offense towards pastors. The devil tried many different ways to build up bitterness, hatred, and offense to prevent me from serving others.

I come from a family of non-educated people. My mother was raised on the cotton farm and my daddy's side of the family was all singers and preachers. My mom quit school in the 8th grade and I believe my dad did too.

More than the education was the relationship with Jesus Christ. I was the first one in my family to go to church and it spiraled to impact the whole family. I got that from my grandmother who prayed for me on her deathbed. She will be in my heart forever!

I've been through a lot, but I'm trusting in a God that healed so many dark places in this bride. After God asked me at the end of my marriage "I want you all to myself for I'm a jealous God", I couldn't step up to the plate on that request. I didn't believe I could be a celibate woman. Why would God want me all to Himself? Well because of my rebellion, I married five more times!

Through the many years of molestation, sexual abuse, rape, and many other painful ordeals; God has taken this Broken Bride and healed her into the Beautiful Bride. I don't look, act, or represent that worldly idea of a beautiful bride; however, to God I'm a beautiful bride and so are you!

These are just a few examples of how the devil tried to take out someone who is destined to serve pastors, marry a pastor, and serve the Bride of Christ and promote them through media such as television, radio and book publishing.

It takes years to overcome patterns and habits that develop from childhood. Some people never seek help to recover from those habits either and that is very sad because we only live once and we should strive to become all that we can be. We should strive to become the best person we can be.

This is what I've tried to do. Although my childhood is very dark and the beginning of my adulthood life was too, I do not let that hold me back from my future. I'm still dreaming. I'm still changing. I'm still seeking. I'm still moldable. I'm still educating myself. I still love. I'm still forgiving. I'm still healing.

We do not give up no matter what happened in our past. I taught my children when they were approaching adulthood to never let circumstances hold them back from their future. Just because I raised them struggling and poor does not mean they have to end up that way. They can get an education. They can fight their way out of the statistics. They can be anyone they set their mind to be! I taught them more than anything to obey God no matter what too!

I pray my story blesses you and encourages you to never give up no matter how many times you fail yourself and God! It's not how you began the race; it's how you finish it!

2
MY LIFE STORY
UNCTION TO DYSFUNCTION

In order to understand why God chose me to write this book about being the Bride of Christ in this hour, you must understand my past and where God has brought me from. At this point in September 2015, I am 47 years old and have been married six times. I came from a very codependent family and was severely codependent myself. Since God gave me this revelation about being His Bride, I've now been single for almost 15 years. The Lord has told me since He gave me this revelation that He is allowing me to marry one more time and now I'm just waiting for that chapter. In the meantime, He's the best husband a woman could ask for! I've been through a lot with Him…and now let me share with you what brought me to this point of full codependence on Him!

Birth to Nine Years Old

My mother comes from a big family of ten brothers and sisters. They were very poor and picked cotton in Arkansas during the summers. My mother's father was a very mean, alcoholic-abusive man. Mom told me stories of how he would beat my grandmother with an iron skillet.

She also told me stories of how they would be pickin' cotton in the field as children, and if they looked up or stood up, they get beaten. Mom recalled a time when she was in the tree picking apples. She remembers looking at a boy for a second and when her dad saw her, he got so mad that he shook her out of the tree until she fell down on the ground. He then beat her for pausing during work!

3

My mother met my dad at 16 years old. They ended up getting married soon after. I think my mother liked dad's sense of humor. He could be very funny when he wanted to be. He was an aspiring country music singer and it intrigued her. He played the guitar and could sing really well.

I don't know much about my father's side of the family except that my father was from Kentucky and he was an alcoholic and mean to my mother. They ended up having four children. I had two brothers and one sister. According to my mother, dad beat mom so many times that she lost four other children. I will be happy to see them in Heaven.

They raised us in Nashville, Tennessee. I was born in Nashville in 1968. The only incident I remember of them being together as a child is him chasing mom around the house with a knife threatening to kill her when I was five years-old. I hid my three-year-old sister under the kitchen table with me. He had a big butcher knife, was drunk, and was running around the apartment screaming for mom. My older brothers were trying to stop him and I don't know where my mom was. I do remember her yelling for my oldest brother to call the police. My sister and I were so scared!

When the police arrived, he held us hostage for a long time. Back then, they could not enter a man's home because it was his castle so he just kept us there.

Devil Molests Me

After that, my mom hid us kids out in Texas with other family members. So, we hid in several states from my dad. Then she hid us at her sister's house in Indiana and during this time we were molested by my uncle.

My sister and I both buried this memory until we were in our mid-20s. At the time I was five-years-old and my sister was three-years-old.

My uncle molested me and my sister for the week and forced me to watch as he molested her.

This traumatized me almost my whole adult life because I ended up always trying to defend the helpless and the ones that could not defend themselves.

4

In my heart I was always trying to make up for what I could not do for my sister. It really hurt too knowing my aunt saw him doing it and didn't stop him.

Years later when these memories came flooding back (when our children became this age of our molestation)...we found out that he had molested all of his children and grandchildren too! He ended up dying by strokes in the nursing home.

By the time we came home...my whole innocence had been taken along with my family. My parents are now divorced and life is ugly.

After this point, my mother became an alcoholic. My mom stayed in the bars (she worked there too) and my oldest brother raised us. At around 8 years old when my father had me and my sister in Florida and he had me sitting on his lap, he went to kiss me and I thought he was just going to kiss me on the mouth or on the cheek but he tried to stick his tongue in my mouth and it grossed me out.

Not long after that incident, I climbed on my mom's dresser and I grabbed the mirror and was shaking it violently as I was screaming, "I hate you! I hate you!" I fell back on the floor and the mirror fell on top of me and cut my face and lip. I still have the scars.

My family knew I had sadness issues but we were too busy surviving that my sister and I never told anyone what happened.

During this time dad was not paying mom child support and she had to take care of us all by herself. Although she would work at the bar all the time, she was a cleaning freak. If she comes home and the house was not clean, she would whip us good (southern explanation).

The Roach House

Right after the divorce when mom was struggling so bad without a man to help her, she moved us in this crappy apartment. It had so many roaches that I am grossed out today thinking about it. There were thousands of them in this house. We would lie in the bed and watch them on the roof. They covered the ceiling. They would fall down on the bed and gross us out. They crawled all over us in the middle of the night. It was just gross.

Well one night my sister went missing. So, FBI came to the house and I was so embarrassed of the roaches. After hours of the police and FBI looking for her, we found her under the covers asleep.

Because of the terror of the roaches, for the rest of my life if I just saw one roach in the house I was in, I was calling pest control. Ugh.

Perfect Mother for an Imperfect Daughter

I remember when I was nine years old and we were living underneath a bar. She came home and I had some candy wrappers on the floor and she was so mad that I had a mess that she smacked me on the face and left a handprint whelp for a week! I wore my hair up on that side of my face when I went to school and the school called the authorities on mom. She was so angry that she held that against me for about twenty years.

Later on she said, "You did that on purpose to get my children taken away from me!" I said, "I probably did do it on purpose. I was probably reaching out for help!"

During this time when she smacked me, we were living underneath a bar that she was managing with her new boyfriend. I remember when I started my period at the age of nine, I ran upstairs while she was working to show her my panties. This is how we lived our lives. The bar was just part of our family.

She would have me sing many times in the bar to the patrons. I remember singing, "Delta Dawn what's that flower you have on?"

We were so poor that the school would take us to get clothes from various charities. At school we were so persecuted over being poor.

The Famous Baseball Story...

I drove buses for over 12 years. I've driven school buses, tour buses and church buses. To entertain my bus riders I would often tell this story:

When I was a little girl we were very poor. We lived underneath a bar and wore hand-me-down clothes.

We lived next door to a family that I called the "rich family". They had both mom and dad and kids always had nice clothes.

We had to catch the bus in their driveway every morning. This home had

two girls, one my age and other one about three years older. I was in the 5th grade.

Well the older sister would beat up on me all the time. One day she asked me, "Would you like to beat up my sister?

I looked at the snobby-acting sister and said, "Actually I would". She said, "Go for it and I won't interrupt." So I went to swing and the older sister beat me to a pulp. So this went on for a good year.

We moved away. Years later I'm playing softball. This Joelton league had teams by color. We were the orange team. The worst team in the league, LOL. Our main opponent was the green team, who was undefeated. Guess who was on the green team? The neighbor who was my age (snobby girl). We were the misfit team.

Well, I was hind-catcher. Close to the end of the season we had a losing record. At this point we were experiencing a losing season. So, we were playing the undefeated green team. We were determined to beat these stuck-up girls! I really wanted to beat them knowing my enemy was on that team.

So here's how fate played out....

We was ahead by one point, last inning, bases loaded, two outs, and guess who was on 3rd base ready to run in....my enemy! So batter comes up to plate and crowd is screaming behind me. I begin yelling, "Batter, batter, batter!"

Strike. I screamed again. Strike. All I needed was ONE MORE STRIKE AND WE WON THE GAME! I screamed again! Swing! Ball flies to center field!

My enemy is storming home and I'm yelling, "Catch it! Catch it!" Well, the ball bounces in front of center-fielder and she catches it and throws it home!

My enemy is sliding foot-first into home plate as I'm jumping in the air to catch the ball. I catch the ball; reach down as her foot is sliding to the plate. I tag her foot BEFORE IT HITS THE PLATE AND THE umpire yells, OUTTTTTTTTTTTTTTTTTTTTTTTTT!!! I'll never forget the sound of that ruling! It means...WE WON! Woohoo!

All of us misfits thought we won the Super Bowl! We were jumping up hugging each other shouting for joy! The green team's parents were shouting

at the umpire saying, "She was safe!" So he was arguing with them over the call. All of the orange team, parents, and coaches were rejoicing over the win! Our coach says, "Go to the concession stand and get a free coke and hamburger on me! I'm so proud of you girls!"

So as we're walking up to the concession stand the green team's parents, coaches, and players were almost rioting behind us. They were SO MAD because they were beat by the worst team in the league! Well I tell the concession stand worker, "I'm here to get my free hamburger and coke." As she's handing it to me, someone said, "June watch out!" I turned around and without thinking twice I went to swinging. IT WAS THE NEIGHBOR'S OLDER SISTER!

She came up behind me to beat me up from behind. But, because I was warned I turned around and got right in the fight. So, we were fist-fighting in the park.

I mean, we were on the ground just punching each other's lights out! All I could remember is her beating me up years ago when I couldn't defend myself. I was older now and could. So they pulled us apart. I tried to walk to the car and she came at me again. We fought again!

Next thing you know, the WHOLE BALLPARK was fighting!

Players, coaches, and parents! The green team was SO MAD so they wanted to fight us! Well, we finally broke it all apart and went to our cars.

I was in my brother's old Ford pickup truck. We were slowly easing out of the park in the traffic and I was sitting by the door. Brian said, "June, here comes that girl with her family (they were walking towards the truck as we were sitting there waiting in traffic); if she calls you a B**tch again, then you get out of this car, I don't care if it's rolling, and you beat her to a pulp!" So...a little later she looked me square in the eye and yelled, "You B**CH!"

8

I saw red. I jumped out of that truck and ran to her. I grabbed her by the hair of the head and slung her head between the bumpers of the cars. My brother jumped out of the truck and made sure no one jumped in. So I beat her good!

I got back in truck and we went home. Her family called us that night and said, "We want to beat up your whole family so meet us at the ballpark tomorrow night!" Yes, we all came and they didn't show up.

Two days later the baseball league punished me and her by benching us a few games. I was so mad because she started it but I took the punishment. At the end of the season they had the awards ceremony. They had all the colors on the baseball diamond and the trophies in the middle. They announced, "Best Pitcher in the League is..." They said, "Best Hind-catcher in the League...June Carpenter!" I was so excited and I went to get that trophy!

Twenty years later I'm coaching cheerleaders in this ballpark. I was talking to the Football commissioner about what happened in this ballpark twenty years ago. He didn't believe me. He thought I was exaggerating. So, the next week he walked up to me and said, "I was at the Barber Shop the other day telling them what a crazy coach I have and the story you told. The barber asked if your last name was Carpenter. I told him it was Knight now but probably was. He told me you were telling the truth because he was the umpire! He said that was the craziest call he ever made." We laughed so hard.

So, for years I told the kids on my buses that fate will play out.

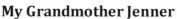

My Grandmother Jenner

I wish I knew my grandmother. The only memory I have is being in the hospital room with her (I was five years old). I remember her asking me to crawl under the hospital sheet with her. She loved on me and prayed for me. She died soon after.

My family always said I had my grandmother's anointing and that I reminded them of her. I can't imagine what my grandmother really went through in her life, but to hear my mother tell it.....it was full of a lot of pain. I'm very thankful she had the Lord to help her through all that abuse.

From what I hear from my family...my grandmother was spirit-filled. She prayed in tongues a lot. I am an intercessor too...so maybe she did impart that to me. I know she's in Heaven praying for me and with me in this journey. :)

After Grandma Prayed...

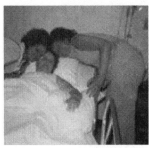

After the encounter with my grandmother in the hospital and her transferring the anointing...I didn't know at the time what really happened. I do remember trying every way I could to get to church. I can remember at 8 and 9 years old being in my old raggedy clothes and standing by the street stopping any church bus that drove by.

If they stopped I would go to church with them. I didn't care what denomination it was...I just wanted to go to church. Sometimes I would take my sister with me.

In those days it wasn't unusual for a young child like that to do things on their own. In today's times they would call the police seeing her stand by the road asking strangers for rides. I'm just thankful that nothing ever happened to me!

I remember going to Baptist, Church of Christ, etc. I remember Christmas at nine-years-old. All I wanted was a bible. I woke up Christmas morning and Santa left me a pretty little pink bible. That was the greatest present!

I remember my drunken father banging on our front door wanting in and me looking at him through the glass door. Mom told us to stay in the house. We were so scared. It was a sad sight. Looking back now....there were so many sad childhood memories.

We were so poor

We lived in this house that didn't have heat. This was in the 70's when hanging sleeves on shirts were in...So I cut my sleeves to hang down so I could look cool. Anyways...we didn't have heat so we had the oven on to heat the house. I was cleaning the top of the stove and my left sleeve caught on fire. I started screaming and my brother put out the fire.

Instead of calling my mother...I called this Christian teacher (I was in 5th grade) and told her what happened. She made me a crochet vest. She was awesome! Anyways...my arm is scarred to this day. The scar goes from my elbow to my wrist. It only shows when I get a tan. Thank God. I know God was with me.

At nine years old I asked Jesus in my heart through Billy Graham on television. I didn't really know what I was doing, but I knew I was hungry.

Anyways...up until ten years old I was seeking the Lord.......

God sent an Angel to Us

During this time my oldest brother is dating a girl named Tammy and she was a godsend to our family! She took us girls to dance classes and this was a great distraction! We took ballet, tap, jazz, acrobats, and then gymnastics! We also played softball! Now, it was extremely rare we ever saw mom at family things, but we were happy to have Tammy. She taught us how to be ladies. She sent us to etiquette classes, etc. She was a dance instructor as well. If it was not for her and my grandmother's prayers......

3
REJECTION FROM A PASTOR

My Encounter with God

At ten years old we had moved in with mom's boyfriend at a cute little house in the country. We only had one church bus that would ride by there. This church was Gray's Point Baptist Church. This church is where I had the true encounter with God as my savior.

I'll never forget walking in the woods by myself. I found a tall stick and felt like I was Moses with his cane pole. I would walk deep in the woods and talk to the Lord like he was my very best friend. I heard his voice clear as a bell. We would talk for hours. I remember sitting on a big rock and just crying about my life. I remember praying for my family. He just loved on me. He was so real to me. I longed to walk in the woods to meet him every day. He was my only friend. I loved feeling the sun shine on my face or the wind blowing my hair. I just always felt close to Him in nature.

During this time, people at school made fun of me because we were poor and I was witnessing all the time. They called me preacher kid. So, needless to say I didn't have any friends. I didn't really care because when I got off that bus, I would go in the woods and meet up with my best friend. He was my comforter. I was never afraid. It was beautiful. I would feel him through the sun shining on my face, the wind blowing in my hair, etc.

The church meant everything to me. I always went. I remember the elders of the church would always tell me, "There's something different about you. You're either going to be a preacher or a missionary."

Rejection from the Pastor

The pastor's 16-year-old daughter was wild. So, when I was around eleven years old, something terrible happened to change my world forever.

One day after church, the pastor asked the congregation if anyone saw his daughter. I replied, "Yes". He inquired as to where she was. I said, "She's outside on the side of the building". He asked, "What is she doing?" I was scared to answer him truthfully. However, I chose to tell the truth and said, "She's kissing a boy."

When I said that, he immediately reacted and kicked me out of the church! He called me a liar in front of everyone and told me to get OUT OF HIS CHURCH! He rejected me! I was devastated! This was my only way to church. I lived to go to church....this was the only sane part of my abused life...

My walks in the woods became less and less....the devil moved in....

Lord I Want to be Popular

In the 5th Grade when the children persecuted me because I was a preacher and serious about my faith, there was one girl in the class that everyone liked. She was the popular girl because she had big breasts. So, at the end of the year I prayed, "Lord, please bless me with big breasts. Thank you." So a few months later when I started the 6th Grade year I had the biggest in the class. The boys just loved me. By the end of the 6th Grade year is when this happened with the pastor rejecting me so it all hit me at the same time.

I quickly realized it was not worth it to be popular for that reason. In the 7th grade I had about 10 boyfriends a day. It became overwhelming and I ended up having to fight all the time due to jealous girls.

Devil Came After My Innocence

At twelve years old the older girls in the neighborhood were jealous of my beauty because the older boys always liked me. The girls tried to pick fights with me. They would make fun of us being poor and call us names. Well, there was this one cute boy who was sixteen years old. He kept flirting with me and one day he took me to a private road with a friend and started kissing me. He told me that when he got done it would bleed a little bit. He took my virginity then he said, "Now you can sleep with whoever you want."

I felt so ashamed after that incident. I just started fighting and cussing all the time. I would defend my sister and I wouldn't let anyone hurt her. I fought all the time. I remember when this older girl walked by and was making fun of my little sister. I stood up and looked her square in the eye (I was in the 6th grade and this was the last day of school).

I said, "Hey you! Pick on someone your own size!" So, when we got off the bus we were standing there cussing each other out. The guy that took my virginity pushed her into me and I had on these cowboy boots that had steel-toes on the end of them. When he pushed her into me, we went round! We were pulling each other's hair and I didn't know how to fight.

I was in self-defense mode. I took that girl by the hair of the head and was banging her head up against the toes of my shoes. I kept kicking her in the face. I was letting all my anger out!

So, she was out of commission for weeks. However, the principal only gave me a paddling because I had never been in trouble and that girl was so much older than me. I was in elementary school and she was in high school.

The next year rolls around and one day the girls at the bus stop were laughing at me and gathered around my purse. Then when I got on the bus, the boy that had sex with me asked me if he could borrow a pencil. So, I reached in my purse to get one and there was a dead snake in my purse! I screamed so loud! All the kids on the bus were laughing at me because they all knew the prank that the older girls played on me. I jumped up out of the seat screaming!

When I went home and told my mother what the girls did, my mom said, "Do you know who put that in your purse?" I said, "Yes." Mom said, "I'm taking you to her house and if you don't whip her a** then I will whip yours!"

So, she took me up the street to her house. I knocked on her door while my mother, her best friend, and my brother Brian and Sheila were in the car waiting. The mother took me down the hallway to the girl.

When I got to her room I said, "Come outside I want to fight you!" She said, "OK." She had a room full of girls. I guess she felt tough.

So, I walked out to the street and stood in the middle and my family got out of their car. This girl comes out (she's about two or three grades older than me too) and she walks out in the street. Her family gathers around and so does the whole neighborhood it seemed like. I confront her about putting that snake in my purse and she begins cussing and I begin cussing. We started swinging and I wrestled her down to where I was sitting on top of her. I had my legs over her arms so that I had her pinned down. I was punching her face as hard as I could and I was saying, "This is for calling me a bit**!" "Don't call me a bit** again!" My brother kept anyone else from stepping in and helping her. I beat this girl to a pulp. All that inside anger comes out on her.

She ended up having to go to the hospital and was out of school for three weeks. I sure made my family proud!

Back in those days, in the late 70s, I remember our school bus driver having a cigarette in one hand and drinking a beer in the other! Yes, driving the school bus! He was always drunk and driving us! He didn't care what we did on that bus! The kids in the back of the bus would be smoking as well!

I also remember going on vacations and mom up front drinking beer with her best friend and smoking cigarettes driving us to Florida! We would be in the back window staring at the stars or laying on the floorboard of the car! We would pee in jugs! We didn't use seatbelts or sit in the seats. The parents would drive drunk and smoke cigarettes with the windows up! It's crazy now that you think about it in today's culture, but back then, this is how it was.

When Barbara Mandrell had a car accident and she was fighting hard to get the seatbelt laws passed, I remember how mad everyone was at her because they would say, "You're not telling us what we can do in our cars!" "We have a right to put them on or not!" It seems funny now because we can't see ourselves riding in a car without one on!

16

Anyways, back to the bus driver driving drunk...I remember this girl coming up and smacking me upside the head from behind and I jumped up and threw her down to the floor and beat the crap out of her while he was driving. He didn't even stop! He just kept going! Crazy huh?

So, while living in the country, I had to fight all the time to survive. We were poor so we were made fun of and because I beat up that first girl, when I got in junior high school, all the tough girls picked on me because they wanted to see if they could beat me up. Also...they would pick on my sister because they knew that made me mad.

In the meantime at the homestead, my mom was living with that man who opened the bar with her, and she seemed to be happy. She was growing a garden and I remember how big that garden became.

We grew everything! I remember her frying everything and even lettuce! She would cook all the time! I also remember we had a dog named D-O-G. Yes, that was his name! Dog spelled out. We always laughed about it.

Family Trips in the 70s - Drinkin' and Drivin' and Barely Arrivin' LOL

I'll never forget the old family trips. My mom was best friends with a lady who had three kids that were our age as well. My mom had four kids but my oldest brother was married at this time. So it was six kids total. Picture all of us crammed in one car.

I remember the youngest boy standing up in between mom and her friend. They would be drinking their six-packs and the boy would drink along with them and he was only three (3) years old. He just loved the taste of beer.

Well the rest of us were in the back seat. I remember the little ones being laid out on the floor board, in the back window and lying down in the seat beside each other. We had jugs in the back seat and we were told to pee in those jugs.

I remember lying in the back window staring at the stars listening to the two young women in the front seat cackling like little girls.

Those two were a hoot. They always smoked their cigarettes, drank their

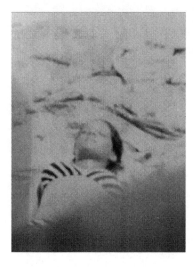

beer and laughed. Mom was the loud-mouth and her friend was the more reserved one. They were best friends through a lot of stuff over the years.

Now back then it was not against the law to drink and drive. Not long after this Barbara Mandrell fought for seat belts and the world went crazy.

Everyone said, "Oh no, that's my constitutional right if I want to buckle up or not!" Society really fought that one. They also tightened the laws on drinking and driving.

I also remember the days in high school and having smoke breaks. All the kids that smoked would go outside and smoke.

So, we arrive in Florida and had a blast! I remember me and her oldest son kissing on the beach under the stars. He was so good-looking! I was probably 12 or 13 at the time. He was my brother's age (3 years older). I also remember him and Brian having fun on the beach. These were the good 'ole days. He passed away when he was in his 20s. He was so young. He had a car wreck on Smiley Hollow Road. Some family members were heading to church and saw him in the field. (They live on Smiley Hollow Rd.). They were with him in his final moments. I'm so thankful for God's timing. This boy was always so full of life.

He's the one that kept the trio of the kid's father and my brother Brian going. He always made them laugh.

The children's grandpa was with him in his final moments...he went to be with the Lord too and now I'm sure they're in Heaven sitting around praying for all of us.

Jenner Family Reunions in Michigan City

My mom was raised in Arkansas and she had like ten brothers and sisters. They all moved to different parts of the United States. However, growing up

I remember the family reunions in Michigan City. All the family would gather from all over America to celebrate family during the summer. I miss these days.

Now, our family was coming from Tennessee. We were southern girls. We were tanned girls. The Yankee boys liked us because we were dark and pretty. They also loved our southern accent.

They used to say, "Talk for us, talk." We used to giggle but loving the attention at the same time. When we went to Michigan City we anticipated seeing our cousins! Anyways...I always loved my cousins because we were all so different.

Family - We are not perfect...but we're Family.

Leaving Poorville for Richville

My mom's boyfriend bought a house in Goodlettsville, Tennessee, which was right on the outskirts of Nashville. It was in a very nice subdivision and was the nicest house we ever lived in. We were so excited to actually be in rich city! This man bought us so many clothes so that we would fit in as we went to the rich school. Although we had nice clothes on, the country girl was still in me! He owned a restaurant in downtown Nashville right on Broad Street. Mom stayed at home and took care of us kids. His mother lived there as well.

Mom seemed so happy at the time except that he wouldn't marry her. I don't know why he wouldn't, but I know it bothered her.

His mother was the only grandmother we ever knew. She would crochet blankets. I enjoyed getting to know her. I remember her always saying that Jesus was coming back before the year 2000. This was in 1980.

I started school in the 8th grade halfway through the year. A couple of weeks later they had cheerleading tryouts for the high school. I always wanted to cheer but had never done it so I tried out.

When I made the squad, the stuck-up girls came over to my desk and said, "Now that we're going to be cheering together, we would like for you to sit with us at lunch." I thought to myself that they had not talked to me since I've been there so I turned them down. This hurt me the rest of my high school career because they blackballed me.

When we got to the high school I loved it! We had rocking pep rallies and I always tried to get our freshman class to win the spirit stick! I would make us signs all week long and get the other freshman fired up, etc. This was the funnest year of my life so far because I was so active and had a lot of friends! Yes, I didn't have to fight all the time! What a new life this was!

I had a home. I had a dad. I had stability. I had nice clothes. I was a cheerleader. My mom stayed at home. I had a grandmother. We had lots of money. It was a great life.

The only thing that bothered me is that this new dad would require us to stand in front of him and pull down our panties for him to whip us. He would bend us over his knee and slowly whip us with his hand. Oh I hated this! I felt funny because of my private parts being exposed to this strange man! Ugh. It just felt perverted!

Other than that…I was very happy! I did get in a fight one time because this girl kept calling me names on the bus and constantly harassed me. So one day I met her when she got off the bus and beat her up. Well I hurt her so bad that she took me to court and when we stood before the judge I showed him all the cruel evil letters she wrote me and brought in witnesses. He ended up rebuking her and told her that she better leave me alone and quit harassing

me! So, I was so happy I didn't get in trouble!

Pictured: My first airplane ride with my mother's boyfriend's mother. She is the only grandmother I knew. I still have a blanket she crocheted for me.

The Stud in a Football Jacket

My brother was a football player at our high school, Beech High School in Hendersonville, TN, and he was three grades ahead of me.

His best friend played football at Greenbrier High School, which was our rival team. One day my brother Brian had this friend over at the house and he walked in the door with that football jacket on and he was so good-looking!

I looked at him and thought, "This is my husband". He said when he saw me in those daisy-duke shorts he fell hard for me too! I was also a very pretty girl and had a great hour-glass shape.

I also stayed dark because I'm part Cherokee Indian so my complexion was always attractive. Anyways, we both fell for each other and started dating soon afterwards. It was funny because I was dating my brother's other friend before this guy came along.

We started seeing each other when I was 14 years-old and he was 16 years-old. My mom saw how close we were getting and she sat me down one day and said, "June, I know his parents. The father abuses the mother and I hate for you to get with an abusive man." Well, me being stubborn, I told her he would never do that to me and that I was in love with him! Boy was I wrong!

21

Halfway through the cheerleading year, my cheerleading coaches pulled me aside in the office and told me I needed to hang around "my own kind."

I asked them what that meant and they said to only hang around jocks. Back then we had jocks (the athletes), the freaks (the dope heads), the frocks (jocks who smoked pot), the nerds (the geeks), the metal heads (heavy metal rockers), then the nobodies (these were the ones who didn't have a classification).

I told those teachers that I couldn't honor that request because I'm not stuck-up and I cannot ignore other people.

Due to that decision, they wouldn't let me try out my sophomore year. I was so sad! I had been to the State Competition saying the Creed for the Future Homemakers of America! I won 2nd place In the State of Tennessee!

After the devastation wore off of not being able to cheer for the school I absolutely loved, I ended up starting Beech High School's very first Pep Club. The school was about 1,200 people and I had almost 1,000 people in the club! The school was so amazed that they put it in the local paper! I was so proud! Anyways I'll never forget the most profound ball game where this club made a big difference!

It was a state playoff game between Beech and Greenbrier!

My boyfriend and my brother going head-to-head their senior year and their possible last ballgame! EPIC! Well my boyfriend was the all-state football player and Beech feared him so much that they decorated their football locker room around this guy! They were like hanging banners saying KILL #00! They feared him greatly. Well since I was dating him, I had a lot

of Beech football players who hated me because of it!

I prepared the Pep Club and we lined up on the football field from one side to the next chanting for the team as they run in on the field and we really showed out to Greenbrier showing school spirit! We ended up winning the game! Afterwards we went to a party and the Beech football players just loved my boyfriend being there. Beech made it to State but lost to Cleveland. See the article.

22

Anyways, right after that my mother's boyfriend ends up cheating on her with a prostitute on Broad Street. He informed my mother that we had to move out and move back to the country house. We were all so devastated because we were so happy.

Not long after moving back to poorville, my mother moves in with another wealthy man and leaves my sister and I alone in this country house. By this time our two brothers were grown and gone. I was 15 and my sister was 13. My mom would come home once in a blue moon and if that house wasn't spotless she would smack us around and scream at us.

So, one day she come home and it wasn't to her expectation and she went to hit me in the face. I was one month away from turning 16. I stopped her hand mid-air and said, "You're not hitting me anymore!" She said, "Well get out of my house then!" I said, "OK."

I had my boyfriend at the house along with my best friend Wendy. So, we all left and my sister was so sad I was leaving her. She hated me for years over that. However, I just couldn't take it anymore.

My friend Wendy and I end up fighting so she goes back to her mom's house. My boyfriend and I are homeless and living out of his car. We end up getting a cheap apartment for $60 a week which included everything (lights

and water). We only had $10 left for the week and that had to pay for food and gas. So, we lived off of beans and cornbread. When we were rich we bought bologna. We would buy one piece of dishes a week until we just built up two of each.

He was a plumber and he would work with his uncle. One week before I turned 16 I called my mother and she tried to talk me into coming home. I said no. Then she said, "I will give you a car." I said, "No. I want to get married." So, she signed for us to get married on my 16th birthday. June 9th.

We got married June 9th, 1984. We were so happy! Two firecrackers who had no idea about love or family, but we had each other!

I stayed home while he worked then I tried to go back to school. I quit high school halfway through my junior year because I needed to go to work to survive.

My First Marriage

I was 16 and he was 18 years-old. I think I had it hell-bent in my mind that if I didn't want to clean my house I didn't have to. I refused to be like my mother. So, that would get on his nerves.

I didn't know it then, but hindsight I see how the little things we did built up to the bigger explosions later on. I don't blame him for the downfall...I blame us both and our pasts. So, when I talk about things that he did, please know that I have forgiven him and he is happily married now and all is well between him, me, and the children. Satan tried to destroy all of our destinies.

The first year of our marriage was pretty good. We didn't have money, but we sure had love and enjoyed making love. We had sex all the time.

It was our bonding experience. However, as the pressures of life rolled on...he started getting mean. A year into our marriage, we separated and I met this man and had sex with him. So, when my husband wanted me back, I told him I couldn't because I cheated on him. I wasn't going to hide it. I was going to tell the truth because we were separated...so I didn't feel guilty.

Well he forgave me and we got back together. Then a couple months later we split up again. I cheated again with another man. Then same thing happened...he forgave me and we got back together.

We then bought our first house and began having children. We tried hard to settle down and have a real family, but his anger and my unwillingness to keep the house decent just made it worse.

4
THE DEVIL MADE ME DO IT

Devil Tried to Kill my First Born & Family

When I was pregnant with Brock, his dad and I were very young and poor.

Luckily, his family threw us a big baby shower. :)

We had no health insurance so we had to give birth at General Hospital in Nashville. I attended Lamaze classes so I had pretty good knowledge of the breathing techniques.

At this time, May 1986, their dad and I lived in these old apartments in Ashland City, Tennessee. I had my bag packed and ready by the front door. It was three days before due date (May 5th). We were at the neighbor's house and we just met them the week before. They invited us over to watch a game and eat chicken. We ate a big bucket of spicy chicken.

After we ate I went to the bathroom and I knew something was wrong. So I walked in the living room to tell my husband that I think we need to leave now that labor is starting. As I was trying to tell him this my water JUST

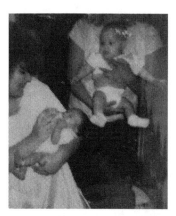

GUSHED OUT! It poured out all over that family's carpet. I WAS SO EMBARRASSED! They weren't upset and were really happy for us.

So we ran down the stairs and we grabbed the bag by the door and a few towels to put under my butt for the car ride. We got in the old Ford Fairmont and put the towels under my butt to catch the water.

It was the funniest car ride I ever had in my life. When he was going so fast and flying around curves, my water would gush out all over the car.

I was like, "Slow down!" Then he would say something to make me laugh. That man had me laughing all the way to the hospital!

Every time I laughed a big pile of water would come up under my blue jeans and roll down my pants to the floor.

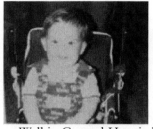

So, we went flying into General Hospital like we was about to die! We didn't know we still had 16 more hours to go, LOL. He went running in the hospital telling them his wife was in labor. They come out with a bed and rolled me into a room.

Well in General Hospital they put you in a room with four other women. I was in a room on the left side by the wall with my legs facing the door (so that anyone walking by could see my privates). Then the other four women were black women facing towards me. It was the funniest thing because I'm over here doing my breathing and calmly in labor while these women were screaming and beating up their men. I laughed so hard! It was funny.

My husband was a trooper! He stayed with me the whole time. I must say I did really well with the breathing until the bearing-down, hard-pressed pains in the end.

Then you can throw the breathing training out the window! I began breathing hard and fast. The problem is that I pushed for three hours! I couldn't get him out!

By this time I didn't care who saw my private parts. Get him out!

Well they told my husband the last 30 minutes that if I didn't hurry up and deliver him (we knew it was a boy)...that they would have to do a cesarean delivery. They rolled me in the delivery room and it was so cold! One nurse practically sat on top of me to push from the top of my belly while the doctor applied forceps to his head and suction cup to pull him out. Come to find out, the cord was wrapped around his neck and every time I would push, it was choking him. So, when I finally got him out, he was dead. He was blue and not moving. When I saw how the doctor was smacking his feet and he wasn't responding I started freaking out so they knocked me out real quick.

I woke up four hours later and as soon as my husband came in the room, I asked him what happened to Brock. He said that they brought him back to life, had to do a blood transfusion and that he was fine. He also said he had all his fingers and toes. I WAS SO HAPPY!

He had to stay in the hospital for about five days but he finally got to come home. Back then we smoked in the hospital rooms. As I recovered I lay in the hospital bed and smoked my cigarettes.

They would finally bring Brock in to visit and I'd get to love on him a while and they would take him back.

In 1986 it was right after they discovered AIDS and being passed through blood transfusions. I made sure I asked the doctors to make sure Brock's new blood was safe. They assured me it was good.

Six months after he was born we were blessed with a new house. We were able to build it and design it all.

Welcome Brock Edward Knight - May 05, 1986.

DABBLING IN THE OCCULT THROUGH OUIJA BOARD

Soon after that I was working again and when I went to pick up Brock at the babysitters, I saw that they were on the Ouija Board. I started playing it and began to be obsessed about it. The board lured me in because it spoke to me the first day about something that only the spirit-world would know. The board told me it was angels from Heaven telling me this information. It is deceiving.

I had all my friends on it and was playing it every day. Some very weird things were happening like curtains catching on fire, etc. I was on this board for a year and a half.

During this time I had another son, Andrew. He was a good birth. He was two weeks late. It was an 8-5 baby. Great birth.

After being on the board for a year and a half, my whites in my eyes started turning red. I wasn't drinking or smoking pot...but they just stayed red all the time. During this time I was hearing voices in my head saying, "Kill your family! Kill yourself! Kill this...kill that." They were always trying to convince me to do something evil. I remember stealing all the time at different stores. I was stealing, lying, etc.

I did everything but cheat on my husband. I believe people that do heinous crimes are demon-possessed. I believe demons are convincing them to do it.

MY DELIVERANCE

By the end of the two months of full-blown demon possession, I was working at my mother's boyfriend's store in the deli. One night I was playing the Ouija Board with someone else in between customers and this eerie, ice-cold presence came in the room. It felt pure evil. It took over the game piece and started talking to us. It said, "I AM SATAN". I mocked him and said, "What if I told you I don't believe in Satan?" He got really mad and started throwing around that piece and said, "You are lying!"

Then a customer come in so I had to hide the board underneath the counter and I didn't close out the board, which meant the spirits you conjured up were still in the room.

(According to legend, you must say bye and close out the board when you play it and to never play it alone).

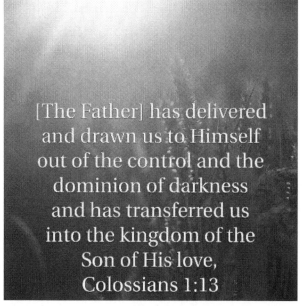

[The Father] has delivered and drawn us to Himself out of the control and the dominion of darkness and has transferred us into the kingdom of the Son of His love, Colossians 1:13

The other woman who was on the board with me started going to the First Assembly of God church and called me and said, "June, I have been praying and I feel to tell you that you must get rid of the board TONIGHT." Well she didn't know I left it at the store. So, I called my sister who was working and told her to have the stock guy burn the board. She said no because she wanted to play it alone that night.

I told her that we had to ask the stock guy to get rid of the board. He tried; however, he had to pour gas on it because it wouldn't burn. It finally burned and left the YES and NO.

The next morning at home I was getting out of the shower at 3 a.m. to be at the deli in the store by 4:00 a.m. When I opened the shower curtain I looked on the mirror and there was the ugliest big demon! It was green, round and had big red eyes. I screamed to the top of my lungs! I didn't know it at the time, but God had revealed what was inside me.

I walk in the bedroom and my husband is lying on the bed reeking in sweat. He said, "Man I've had the worst nightmare! I dreamed I was fighting thousands of snakes.

I kept throwing them off me but they kept surrounding me. I could hardly breathe!" I didn't know it at the time either that he was fighting demons in his sleep. Apparently I stirred up the devil the night before and he was wreaking havoc in our home!

So I get to work and my mom walks in and she says, "Oh my God! You look demon possessed! Your eyes are bulging out of your head! Go to a Pentecostal church and cast them out!" I started crying and told her about the demon I saw on the mirror that morning and that I was possessed and I needed help. I didn't know what a Pentecostal church was. I called all of them in Ashland City and none could help me. So, I ended up talking to a Baptist pastor who said, "Ma'am, what's a Ouija board?" I said, "Sir, it's a medium that you conjure up spirits with." He said, "OK, well meet me when you get off work."

So, for the rest of the day the demons were so mad! They kept telling me how they're going to kill me. They told me not to be alone that they would catch my hair on fire, make my head spin, cut my head off, etc. Just lots of gross stuff!

So, my eyes got redder as the day went on. I talked my sister into going with me to the Baptist Church after work. She said, "I'm scared of you. Just please don't look at me." So, in the car I looked in the rearview mirror as we were heading out and I said, "Look at my eyes!" She screamed, "NO!" I said, "No, look, they're solid white. The devil is trying to make me look like a liar and a crazy person so they will lock me up! She couldn't believe it either! However, the closer we got to the church the redder my eyes got.

I was crying so hard because the devil was telling me he was going to kill me for doing this. So, I asked my sister to take care of my kids for me when I died. I seriously thought he was going to kill me. When I pulled up into the church's driveway, it was a long driveway and a shadow fell on me in the car. It hit me from the top of my head and went to the soles of my feet. It was pure darkness. The devil spoke to me and said, "If you go in that church, I will make it fall in on you and kill you!"

So, when I got parked I slammed that door open and ran in the church! I ran in the pastor's office screaming, "HELP ME! HELP ME!"

He said, "Ma'am, did you bring it with you?" I said, "The board?" He said, "Yes." I said, "Sir, you don't want that in a church."

It is evil." So he began asking me questions. He said that he had done some research since we got off the phone and he asked me, "Ma'am, have you been lying?" I said, "Yes". I was wondering how he knew.

He said, "Have you been stealing?" I said, "Yes sir..Many times." All the questions he asked I had done except cheat on my husband. So, he put the bible at the end of the desk in front of my face and he sat it up facing me. He said, "Does the devil have more power than this bible?" You would think it would be so easy to say, "No, you know he don't." But, I couldn't answer him because all I could hear was a bunch of screaming demons in my head saying, "YOU KNOW I HAVE MORE POWER THAN THAT BIBLE! YOU KNOW I DO! YOU KNOW I DO!"

So, while all the screaming voices were going on, I heard a voice I haven't heard in 10 years. It was that still small voice I heard in the woods when I was ten years old. This voice said, "June, it's time to come home." When I heard God I grabbed that bible and started crying uncontrollably saying, "Save me God, save me!"

So I said the sinner's prayer. I went to church there a couple of weeks but I was so bored. It didn't do anything for me.

It was so boring! I just quit going. Well my old friend that told me to get rid of the board invited me to the Assembly of God church because they were preaching on the Book of Revelation and I love end times subjects so I told her, "I will go but I'm wearing blue jeans and if they say anything to me about it I'm walking out!"

So, I went on that Wednesday night and half the church was in blue jeans. I had met my destiny that night.

Old Man Casts Demons Out

I got saved six (6) months before I turned 21. My son Andrew was born during this time. The first night at the Assembly of God church I met this old man in the church (I love wise old men) and asked him if he heard of a Ouija board. He said yes, grabbed the anointing oil and cast the devils out. I never heard voices again and was delivered of lying, stealing, etc. I felt those demons leave!

A month later I got delivered of smoking cigarettes! God changed my life in that church. After I got delivered, I brought all the ones that I encouraged to dabble in the Occult with me.

For years following my deliverance, I traveled and cast demons out of people and houses. God used me to deliver others trapped by the devil.

Our First House

We built this house when I was 18 years old. We were married for two years. We had the privilege of designing the floors, cabinets, etc. We were able to get this house through the FHA government loan; First-time buyer program.

We were so excited about this house because it was our future being built. I can imagine how it made my husband feel like a real man...he's providing a home for his family. Our past was so rocky...this was our American dream.

So many memories in this home. We lived here for about five years. Brock was six months old and we moved in right before Christmas of 1986. Andrew and Meagan were both born while we were living in this house.

We had many a good Christmas' and holidays in this home. I also remember us whipping the kids with a wooden paddle. If you were to ask the kids about this paddle they would tell you they remember it. They ended up hiding the paddle and I found out years later they hid it under the stairs, LOL.

During this time at this house I started going to First Assembly of God Ashland City. Our pastor was awesome! He helped me and my mom find Jesus in such a real way. We ended up filling up rows with people. We would take people from Bearwallow Road. My mom always cared about the less fortunate.

Ice Storm of 1992

This house was located on a hill. I will never forget the winter of 1992. It was the biggest ice storm I could ever remember. We had this old potbelly wood stove in our unfinished basement. My husband would put wood in the old wood stove and open the door upstairs and it would warm most of the house. He cut the wood and keep it in the basement.

During this Ice Storm, we were without electricity for three weeks. We had to survive in the basement with just the wood stove.

I remember him cooking bacon on that old stove. It smelled so good. Even while we were in the basement with the kids, you could see out the windows and see ice hanging all over everything. The ice was so thick that it was popping the trees right in half! It sounded like firecrackers going off! It seriously sounded like we were in a war.

He tried I don't know how many times to get up the street in his truck and he couldn't get passed the ice. We were stuck. However, God took care of us.

My First Home, 108 Katie Court, Ashland City, TN 1986

My 1st Experience with Holy Ghost

After I got saved at the Ashland City First Assembly of God when I was 20 years old, I started noticing how people acted strange like speaking in this weird language and shaking at the alters. I was raised Baptist and Church of Christ so I was not used to Pentecostal. I was actually taught it was the devil. But, since the Baptist didn't know what to do with me when the devil had me in a stronghold (possession), and the Pentecostals cast him out (the devil)...then I knew they were real.

One day I was watching this woman at the altar. She was on the floor knelt at the altar praying.

Next thing you know her right shoulder started twitching. Then it moved to her left shoulder, and then she stood up. She started dancing. I never saw this type of behavior before and it amazed me. I asked my friend, "Is something wrong with that girl? She's twitching weird."

My friend replies, "No, she just has the Holy Ghost on her." I was a dancer growing up so I love dancing. She threw her hands around and danced very intimately and passionately. I knew she was doing it before the Lord.

I watched her as I was crying and I said to the Lord, "I want to do that one day." The next thing I saw was people speaking in such a beautiful language. It sounded like they were speaking in foreign languages.

I asked the old man that cast them demons out of me, to explain what this "Holy Ghost and speaking in tongues" means. He explained the periods of time like God in the Old Testament, Jesus in New Testament and the Holy Ghost to finish out the end times. He explained that I need Him to give me the power to live in Christ.

So I went home and prayed about it. Next Sunday Pastor asked the church after worship if anyone wanted to get prayed for anything. I went up there. (This was my husband's first day in church. He saw how different I was since I quit Ouija board, smoking, etc.). I told Pastor at I wanted to be filled with the Holy Ghost if it's real. So pastor called the elders of the church up.

They laid their hands on me and prayed in tongues. I felt this shining light shine over me and hit my head. When this light hit me it was burning hot. It went from the top of my head to my feet. I began shaking and my tongue went crazy.

It was speaking this weird language but it was only two syllables, not like the full languages I heard from the others. I was burning in his glory and was shaking all over! It was polar opposite of what happened when I was demon-possessed and the dark shadow fell over me from the top of my head to the crown of my feet and told me it was going to kill me if I went to see that pastor for deliverance.

Also, I'd like to point out how that when Satan entered the room on the Ouija board how eerie and ice-cold the room became. With darkness it's icy cold and with God it's burning hot. It seems weird considering Hell is a burning flame. Hmm.

Back to the infilling of the Holy Ghost: I turned around to face the church and go back to sit with my husband and I felt like my face shined to the whole church. I felt like Moses must have felt when he left the glory on the mountain. I could feel the Lord in every fiber of my being!

I sat down beside my church and I know it freaked him out. My pastor said, "June, I guess you got filled with the Holy Ghost today huh?" I laughed and said, "Yes sir!" The church laughed.

After this experience I began operating in the gifts of the Holy Ghost and began ministering to other people. I traveled singing gospel music, visited prisons, cast demons out of houses and people, and did crazy things like obey the Lord as I'm driving down the road and He would give me directions to go to a certain house to pray for a stranger, etc.

My Mother's Salvation Story

At the time when I got saved, mom was living with that wealthy man and helping him to manage his stores. He owned three businesses. One gas station by the interstate, one grocery store, and a video store. So, she was still an alcoholic and drank probably a case of beer a day or at least a 12-pack. She was totally addicted. So, when I went back to church and she saw how God had delivered me from smoking three packs of cigarettes a day and how I had quit cussing, got delivered from demons, etc., then the Holy Ghost started convicting her.

I would invite her to church and she would always make excuses. Well there was a revival coming up and she promised to go.

When she woke up that Sunday morning, instead of going she opened up a can of beer and got wasted drunk that day. The next morning she felt so guilty that when she was working in the store at 4:00 a.m. she told the Lord, "God, if you will help me not to drink when I get off work, I will go to the revival with June." The devil spoke back and said, "If you go to church with June you will starve to death. You will lose your job and lose everything."

God helped her not to drink. When she arrived at the church she said that it felt like a big hand grabbed her heart. The pastor preached right to her then when it came time for the altar call you could see her standing there shaking battling going down there. So I looked at her and said, "He's been waiting for you."

She said when she went down there she cried so hard because the biggest weight was lifted off her shoulders. Once she went back home she quit drinking. God instantly delivered her from alcohol addiction at the altar.

So, now she's going back to living with this man and she knows God does not approve of that lifestyle. She had been battling this thing for weeks because she knew the price she would have to pay to get things right with God.

At the time, she was living with the man she worked for. She was driving his big nice Cadillac and everything she had was in his house. He took her on very nice vacations and she traveled all the time in his motor home. By getting right with God she knew she'd have to give up all this luxury to honor God.

After she got saved that night, she went back to the revival the next night and gave up her cigarettes! God instantly healed her! She went to church every time the doors were open. Well, the boyfriend didn't like this new woman so he told her no watching preaching in his house, etc. So, she ended up moving out one day while he was out of town. He comes home to an empty house. She kept telling him that she was leaving him and quitting her job. She told him he had two weeks to find someone to replace her.

He didn't believe her so when the time came, she moved out and didn't show up at work. They called him and said no one was at the store and he had to rush to cover her. So, when she left him she went back to the old country house. She was so happy alone with God. He was talking to her through the word and she would play worship music all the time.

At church pastor would preach for like six weeks on how we are not to be unequally yoked. Mom always knew it meant that she cannot go back to the rich, unsaved man. Well one day he showed up at her house and said, "I will marry you if you give up your religion." She said, "No." So, he left.

Then he came back the next week and said, "I will marry you even if you keep your religion." So she asked him to go see her pastor with her. Now, here's this pastor that has been preaching to not be with someone if you're unequally yoked, however, when he found out how wealthy this man was, it changed his mind. (Just my opinion). The reason I assume this is because I had just met with him a week before mom did and told him that the only reason my mother was battling so much about marrying him is because he's so wealthy and it's security for her and he asked who it was. Well, everyone in this town knew this man.

So, my mother brings this man to see the pastor and the pastor gives his approval for them to get married. They went to the Justice of the Peace.

I couldn't believe it! I knew it was a trap! Once they got married, he shut off all money to her, she ended up moving into the basement and he wouldn't allow her to watch any preaching or do anything Christian in HIS home. It was a trap through and through. This lasted about three years then they ended up divorcing.

I remember my mom listening to a three-way radio hiding under the covers just to hear the word of God. She was so hungry!

This was over 30 years ago and she never married again. God has taken care of her ever since and she never backslid! He ended up marrying another woman and is very happy. One night last year I had a dream and the Lord told me to get up and go see him at the store. He told me he would be there and I had to confess to him about stealing from his store 30 years ago when I worked for him and while I was on the Ouija board. Well, I woke up and went to see him and he was there! He was shocked to see me after 30 years. I told him what the Lord said in the dream and I repented to him. Do you know that man cried and thanked me for being honest! I told him I would work it off what he thought was good recompense and he said I didn't have to. I also prayed over that building to cast the demons out that I left there from the Ouija Board. I also told him that the Lord said He will bless his business now. So, it all worked out.

The Three Hungry Women

So, from the very beginning, it was mom, me and this other woman from church named Wanda. We were all so hungry for more of the Lord and we were the shouters and the amen corner. We would go to conventions of Benny Hinn, etc. We did prayer meetings on Bearwallow Road and people got saved, healed and delivered all the time. Wanda was always a gifted preacher. She was the prophetic one.

Mom had the gift of healing. Her hands would burn like they were on fire and she knew someone was there that God wanted to heal.

She would lay hands on them and they would get healed! I was the one of the deliverance. I cast demons out of people all the time because of where I came from.

I have so many stories to tell of how God used us, but I will tell a funny story of how desperate or dumb we were. We were visiting Clarksville First Assembly of God on a Sunday morning and we were running late. Wanda was driving and going like 70 mph on a 55 mph highway. Well we got pulled over and the officer said, "Ma'am did you know you were going xx amount of miles over the speed limit?" She said, "Yes officer, we are running late to church." Man we laughed about that for years. We have so many good memories of us together, especially at Sister Gladys' house in Clarksville.

Brock's First Healing

When Brock was four years-old, his grandma believed in miracles. She had the gift to pray for people and they would be healed. One day Brock got very sick. (I don't remember the sickness).

Maw-Maw laid hands on him and he was slain in the spirit (laid on the floor). He woke up and was miraculously healed!

Brock said, "Praise the Lord! I'm healed maw-maw!"

My Miracle Baby

I was not saved when I was pregnant with my two boys. After I got saved I prayed one night and asked the Lord to please give me a little girl before he came back in the Rapture.

A few months later I found out I was pregnant. I was working at the United Methodist Publishing House in Downtown Nashville. I began seeing the doctor and he noticed something was wrong.

He suggested we get an amniocentesis test. I was so nervous. Her dad and I went to get the test and the needle was like eight (8) inches long. It was so scary! They stuck that long needle in my stomach.

I didn't feel it too much until it got in her amniotic sack. Then it was like someone stabbing me from the inside out.

The doctor informed us that it will take a couple of weeks for the results. He also suggested that if it comes back that the baby had a crooked spine that we consider an abortion. I told him that we are Christians and don't believe in that. We believe God can heal the baby.

So, I prayed for two weeks diligently for this baby. During these two weeks, Jesus came to see me in a dream. I was in Heaven and surrounded by clouds. Out of the clouds Jesus walked up to me and said, "June I gave you the girl you asked for. She is healthy. Don't worry. I love you." I said, "Thank you Jesus." He said more things, but I can't remember what He said. I didn't write my dreams down back then.

When the call came in the doctor said, "Well, you're having a healthy baby girl! Congratulations!" Man, I shouted, started crying and ran to the bathroom. The bathroom was across the street from the president's office and they come running in there wanting to know what was wrong. When I told them the good news they rejoiced with me!

She ended up being a late baby too. She was born two weeks late and weighed 9 lbs. ¼ ozs. She was a healthy baby girl. As soon as she was born, my mother and husband were in the room with me. I was crying and thanking Jesus for my beautiful baby girl.

Our pastor from First Assembly of God was there to pray for her. She was blessed the moment she entered Earth.

Welcome Meagan June Knight 06/15/91.

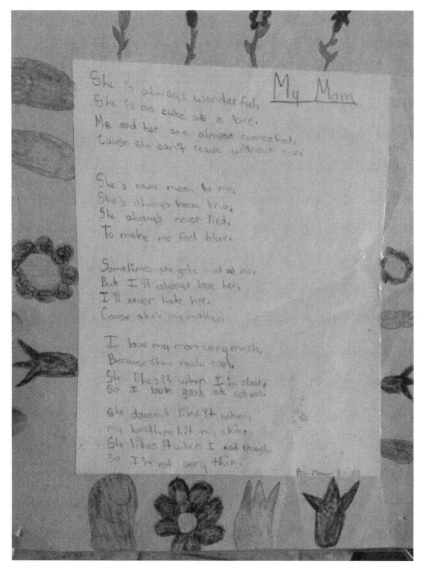

The Rejection from Another Pastor

When I was attending First Assembly everything was going great until I started working with the youth. I would take some youth to Clarksville First Assembly because they had an awesome youth pastor. On Saturday nights they would do street witnessing and do prayer before they went out on the streets.

So, I would bring the youth up there and we partnered with them and tore up Clarksville! This church in Clarksville had the best youth pastor around!

He was so on fire for God and developed an outreach service before we hit the streets that just took us all in the throne room. By the time we hit the streets we were in the presence of the Lord and on fire! We all admired him greatly for his passion and fire.

I Heard God's Voice Audible

So, one day I had three girls in the car with me as we were traveling to Clarksville to partner with this youth group. It was at night and we were listening to worship music down low and it was a woman singing. Next thing you know a man's voice, very authorative, comes in the car and says, "JUNE". I thought I was hearing things so I looked at the girl in the seat next to me and she started crying. She said, "Did you hear that? It called your name." So, since I knew I was not crazy, I turned around to the girls in the backseat and was asking them if they heard the man's voice. They said they did not hear it. So, the girl in the front seat said that she heard it call my name again but I didn't hear it the second time.

I pulled the car over on the side of the road, got out and stood on the side of the road and said, "God, if that's you trying to talk to me, what do you want to say?" He didn't reply. So, I got back in the car and drove on to the church. This night was different. I felt the power of God all over me. When we got to a mall there was a bunch of youth standing around a car and they were blasting rock and roll music. So, I said, "Lord, shut their radio off so we can witness to them." Next thing you know, their radio stops! It opened the door for us to go minister to them!

So, these weekly trips to Clarksville changed our youth group because it instilled hunger in their hearts for more of God.

Back to the Rejection

I planned a weekend slumber party for about twelve girls because our church was having revival on Sunday. I figured we would play games, pray and we would get to know each other. Man did we have fun. I ended up telling them my life story and we talked a lot about Heaven.

We all cried together and some of the girls got healed from abuse, etc. It was a great weekend.

So, Sunday rolls around and we all got up and got dressed to go to revival. We filled up two rows at church. The evangelist preached on, "Is your name written in the Lamb's Book of Life?" So, after bowing my head at the altar time I looked up and ALL the girls were at the altar giving their life to God! These girls were from the high school and not saved!

So I started shouting and running around that church! I went crazy!

The next week we had a testimony service and the pastor got so mad at me because I was so highly favored with the youth and their parents.

A lot of the girls that got saved started bringing their family members to church, etc. Due to the parents standing up praising me for all the hard work I had done with their kids and how their lives were being changed, the pastor called me in his office and kicked me out of the youth. So, being that I wasn't the youth pastor…they severed that. He told me to back down and don't have anything to do with the youth anymore. I was devastated. So, I only stayed at that church about a week or so more.

Jesus Comes to See Brock & Fills Him with Holy Ghost

Brock was five years-old and we started attending the Faith is the Victory Church in Nashville, TN. It was on a Wednesday night. Brock was in the back in their Children's Church. Their Children's Church program was setup like an adult church. They had worship, preaching, teaching, crafts, etc.

This night I went to pick him up from the class and when I grabbed his hand he said, "Momma, I saw Jesus tonight." I said, "You did? Well tell me about it in the car." So, we go out to the car and I began to inquire as to his

experience. He said, "They told us about Jesus and I went forward to get saved. They prayed for me momma and I fell on the floor." I laughed (we call it slain in the spirit when you get prayed for and fall back under the power of God).

He continued, "When I was on the floor Jesus came to see me. He talked to me but I do not remember what he said.

43

Now my tongue won't stop tickling."

He spoke in tongues for two days. I remember the glow on his face. He couldn't stop speaking in tongues. We filmed him but lost it over the years.

Brock Saw Santa Claus

When my kids were little, we had this family tradition:

On Christmas Eve we went to mom's house and would exchange gifts with the other family. When we got home the kids would open one present from mom and dad before bed.

The kids would also put the cookies and milk out for Santa Claus.

Well this one Christmas we were living in our very first house. Brock was about five years-old, Andrew was three and Meagan was six months old. Brock and Andrew shared a room with a big bunkbed. Brock slept on the bottom full-size and Andrew on top on the twin size. Meagan had her own room.

We had the Christmas tree in the living room and all the presents under it awaiting the kid's Christmas morning joy.

So this particular Christmas morning their dad and I had been up about all night putting their toys together and only had a couple hours sleep. We waited and waited for the kids to get up and they just kept sleeping. So me and their dad come up with the bright idea to trick the boys.

I had this bell necklace and their dad took that necklace and put it by the boy's bedroom door. He banged on the door real hard, shaking the bell and yelled (like Santa Claus), "Ho Ho Ho! Merrrrrrrrrrrrrrry Christmas!"

44

We could hear Brock jump up out of bed yelling, "I see Santa Claus...look Andrew, he's leaving our roof on the sleigh!" "Andrew...get up! Santa Claus just left!" Me and their dad were standing outside the door rolling!

We ran back to the living room and sat down like we didn't do anything. LOL. Boys come running in there SO EXCITED FOR CHRISTMAS! Man...those were the days! Brock proclaimed for years that he saw him!

The Husband's Experience With God

So, I started going to Clarksville where the fire was. There was a group of us that always went to Sister Gladys' house for prayer meetings. Well, my husband came one night and God met him there. He got slain in the spirit and started speaking in tongues and crying his heart out. I mean he was weeping.

When he came up off the floor, he was greatly repenting to me for all the hell he put me through. All the way home he was repenting for all the sorrow he had caused me. I was crying too because I had been praying for him for years and was so happy. So...I was happy about the conversion!

When we got home, we prayed and anointed the house with oil and told those demons to leave! We cleaned that house out! We also made the best love that night.

Well, the next morning he went to work so happy about his new life. However, he came home a different man.

He said, "Never again!" I said, "What do you mean?" He said, "Never again and I'm doing what I did last night! I was made fun of all day. I'm not living like that! NO." He was very serious and had his mind made up.

Now Devil Tries to Get Dad to Kill First Born & All Of Us

Since that time, he became seven times worse with anger than he was before. Over the years he beat the animals and I can't even write about some of the things he did to animals. I'll just give one example. We had this cat, and he hated cats. He would throw that cat around and kick it around, scream at it, etc. Well the cat ended up peeing in his shoes just to make him mad. So when he caught the cat doing that, he took it by the tail and slammed it against the walls. He slammed him all up and down the hall. Then he stepped on his head and neck until poop come out his butt.

The cat died a couple of weeks later where its stomach swelled up because he couldn't' pee anymore. Just stuff like that. Horrible.

Then he would turn the lights off in the house and terrorize us. He would chase me and the kids through the house screaming and making noises, etc. It was just demonic. Then he would kick the kids across the room (the boys).

My Precious Andrew

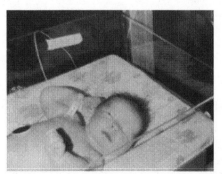

One night I was in the bedroom and I heard him yelling at the boys and the next thing you know I heard this loud thump. I knew in my heart that he kicked one of them across the room. He was mad at them because they were being boys and not going to sleep.

So, I rushed in there and saw the two boys lying in the bed shaking. It was so sad. I'm crying just remembering this. Anyways, I said, "What happened?" He confessed what he had done and I got so mad at him!

My son Andrew always got the worst of it from his dad. I don't know why

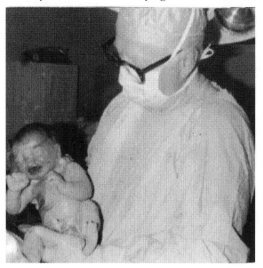

he did but I think it's because he always defended me. When his dad would do something to me Andrew would say, "Dad, don't do that to momma." He would tell him to shut up. Well, Andrew finally got to where he would get so mad that he would hold his breath and turned blue while lying on the floor. This is when he would get so mad at his dad.

Andrew Wayne Knight born May 24, 1988 in Nashville, Tennessee

For a long time I thought that Andrew had hearing problems and I took him to specialists, etc., but come to find out, he would just zone out. He would be thinking about something and he would be in his own world. However, due to this it did open the door to him going to Head Start at four years old, which became an advantage to his education.

Here's more about Andrew:

I forget how old Andrew was at this birthday party, but he had to be about 10 or 12. We had it at a skating rink and he had all his friends there skating. The whole baseball team was there enjoying the race on the court. Next thing you know, Andrew fell and broke his finger.

So he comes over to me and shows me this sideways finger. I freaked out and said, "Sorry friends, I have to take him to emergency room." Even though he was in all that pain, he made me laugh all the way to the hospital.

This is so typical of Andrew's personality. Andrew always made his momma laugh.

I remember him in the house cleaning and doing impersonations of Elvis or Johnny Bravo. He's say, "Woah Momma, Woah Momma." I'd laugh so hard!

One time Andrew was doing a skit in front of the church and he was acting like that jungle guy who would wrestle crocodiles. So, Andrew was wrestling this air toy crocodile and he said, "Wow, you are cranky! Must be that time of month." I laughed so hard but the church didn't think it was funny. He got in so much trouble over that comment. We still laugh about it to this day.

Also, Andrew was the only child out of the three that never left me. He never wanted to go live with his dad. He stood by my side through thick and thin. Also, later on in his teenage years, I believe God rewarded him for being so good and faithful to his mother. I don't know what I would have done without my precious Andrew.

Back to Marriage Story

I kept praying for him to be healed and delivered and I brought the kids with me to church and I tried everything to save our marriage. I went to the pastor and asked him what the bible said about abuse and he just gave me videos to watch.

When my husband found out I told the pastor…he was very angry. The last year we were married, he kept telling me he was going to kill us all the time. He would tell me various ways to kill us. He was a pure redneck…a mean one. He didn't drink so he didn't have any excuses to be so mean. Please hear my heart in that I'm not saying I'm perfect. I had stubborn ways too and we were just two bombs together ready to explode because of our childhood. We didn't know how to be parents, much less what a healthy relationship meant!

Dream about Husband Cheating

After our daughter was born, I had a dream. I saw my husband on the job and that he had cheated on me with three women. I saw how they happened and what they looked like. One was at a bar, one was on the job and the other was something else (can't remember).

So, I woke up afterwards and it woke him up because I was so upset. I told him about the dream and he said, "Go back to sleep... the dream is not true."

So I went back to sleep rebuking the devil and the next day I couldn't stop praying in tongues in intercession. I knew it was over my husband but didn't know what about. I forgot about the dream.

So, he comes home from work and I confront him and say, "I've been praying in the spirit all day and something tells me you need to repent about something.

I've been praying for you all day." So, he begins to confess that he had cheated on me with three women exactly how God told me. So, I forgave him.

How I Changed in This Marriage

Well, besides the fact that I was raised being abused and was used to this type of behavior...it was from a man and not a woman. I didn't have a father and all the men in my life were not good examples. So, when he would yell and get mad it would make me shake and be so terrified. He was like 6'1 260 lbs. He was solid muscle.

So, during this marriage I gained 150 lbs. Within nine years I became twice as big as I was when we married. Growing up I was never overweight. I was very athletic and never bigger than a size 12 and 140 lbs.

At the end of this marriage I was 300 lbs. and a size 28. Of course I'm not blaming him for it, but it was just how I chose to deal with the stress of this marriage.

Also, it didn't help him that I was not a good housekeeper. However, one thing he can't say is that I wasn't a good mother and wife as far as other things. I fed them good and took care of my children.

I believe the house cleaning thing was due to my mother's abusive behaviors when it came to having a spotless house. She was just ridiculous if you had one thing out of place. So, I guess after being hit so many times I just chose to live a little and not let it ruin me or treat my kids like that. My problem was that I went to the other extreme about it.

I remember one time that my husband's family came to visit and I was so embarrassed. The house was so messy that you couldn't walk through it.

There were things on the floor and everywhere. It wasn't filthy but was just extremely messy.

Anyways…I was very embarrassed. After our divorce my mother told me that the reason my husband was so mean to me was because I didn't keep a clean house. Maybe so, only God knows. Like I said, I'm not totally blaming him for the marriage…we both had issues for sure.

Went to California to Lose Weight

My husband would tell me all the time that he was divorcing me if I didn't get this weight off. He told me all the time how disgusting, fat, ugly and horrible I had become. I tried everything to lose weight but nothing would work. I tried Weight Watchers, Jenny Craig, etc.

One day I was watching TV and a commercial came on saying 1-800-HELP-4-ME. It was a Christian Counseling place in Van Nuys California. So, I called them and told them that I had gained 150 lbs. in this marriage and my husband was going to divorce me if I don't get it off and could they help me.

I had never been through serious counseling so I didn't know what to expect but I was desperate to save my marriage.

The place took my insurance information and flew me out there the next day. This trip saved my life. I was there for three weeks and when I told the group therapy meetings the abuse I was living in they opened my eyes to how abusive it really was. They helped me to see how grave in danger I was….and my children.

I called my husband and told him that if he didn't come out there for counseling and to get help that I was divorcing him.

Well, he flew out there for a week and when he came home at first it was great. It wore off after a couple of weeks and he went back to his old ways.

5
GOD IS JEALOUS OVER ME!

Instruction from God

Right before I left the Counseling Center in California, I was laying on the couch in intercession to God. I knew we were probably going to divorce if he didn't change his patterns. So during the intercession I heard God's voice and He said, "I want you all to myself for I'm a jealous God." I thought I wasn't hearing Him right so I said, "What did you say?" He said it again, "I said, I want you all to myself for I'm a jealous God." I said, "Are you saying I can never get married again?" He replied, "I want you all to myself." So, I said, "No God. I can't be like that. You know all I wanted since I was a little girl was to have a family. I never had a dad. Why would you ask me to give up having love and a family?" So, I disobeyed Him. I was way too codependent for that!

The First Divorce

When I came back to Tennessee I started going to another church. We started at Faith is the Victory Church. At this church Brock was five years-old and got filled with the Holy Ghost on a Wednesday night in Children's Church. I write about this later.

Well after that experience, the pastor interrupts his sermon on a Sunday night and he says, "I don't know who this is for, but there's someone in here, you're living in abuse, and if you don't get out your husband could kill you." Then he went back to his sermon. I KNEW IT WAS FOR ME! I had been praying for him for five years! The Lord spoke to me right then and said, "You don't have to live in that anymore." I wanted to shout! I was free!

So, on the way home, the children were all under six years old so they knew to be quiet while mom was praying in tongues. I was doing warfare over something! I didn't know what it was! It was on a Sunday night and I had a 30 minute drive getting back to the house. I was beating on the steering wheel warfaring over something.

Well, when I walked in the house with the kids I knew what it was. Satan was waiting for me on the couch! He had it set in his heart that he was going to kill us that night. God warned me at church, had me pray against the attack, and prepared my heart for the attack.

I put the kids to bed and prayed in the spirit coming back down the hall to the living room because I knew he was going to abuse me. You always know when they're going to. You can just tell by the look in their eyes.

In my heart I was begging God to help me.

When I sat on the chair across the room from him he started in on me. He began calling me names and putting me down. Previously I'd cry and he would wear me out. He told me things like, "You're so fat, I'm embarrassed to be seen with you, you think you're goody-goody-two-shoes, you think you're better than me because you're a Christian?"

He knew this time was different because instead of him wearing me down, I just replied like this, "Hallelujah. Thank you Jesus. God is good." It made him even madder when he wasn't wearing me down. So after two hours of putting up with this, he gets up to go to bed and he says, "Let's go to bed." I said, "I'm not sleeping with you anymore."

I can remember many times he would rape me if I tried to say no. so…you never said no to him. So, when I said no, he slammed me on the couch and began attacking me from the front. I fought him back for the first time. I was kicking him on the back and we were going round! When he got done he stood up and said, "I'm going to get the shotgun and I'm going to blow you and the kids heads off while you're sleeping tonight. I'm going to kill you all." He was dead serious too.

I rolled over and had a flash back of my dad trying to kill my mom with a knife 20 years ago! (I was 25 at this time). I was like, "Wow, you married someone just like your dad." It was a revelation.

So, I just prayed that God would send angels and protect me and the children. I pled the blood of Jesus over us.

We made it to the next morning! God saved us!

So, he came in the living room saying, "I don't know what came over me. I'm so sorry; I won't do it again, etc." After he went to work, I went to the courthouse and went to see a judge. I filed an Order of Protection against him. The judge read what I wrote and told me to go into hiding.

He signed papers granting the kids permission to be out of school. I went into hiding for three weeks then my husband found me. He called and said that he wanted a divorce or he was going to prison. So I told him I wanted the house, car, kids and everything in the house.

He agreed. So we divorced.

The problem was my family. They blamed me for the divorce and told me that I had a good man that provided me with a brand new home, brand new car, and I should just put up with it. He's the kid's father, etc.

So, everything was my fault to them. I wasn't a good enough wife is why he acted like that.

So, I met this man and fell in love. My family hated him because he was oneness Pentecostal. He was Jesus Only.

More Rejection from Pastors

Remember when I wrote about my experience as the ten year-old girl who was kicked out of the church by the pastor because of his wild daughter, well 15 years later after my divorce I was substitute teaching at Cheatham County High School. God was really moving in that school. He just opened the door for me to testify to the children about how God delivered me out of the occult and witchcraft. I told them how God had delivered me out of abuse, etc.

Many miracles happened in this high school. The pastor of that old Baptist Church approached me one day and asked me if I would consider being the youth pastor of his small church because he only had about three youth there but he wanted his church to grow. He saw my anointing with the youth and he wanted it at his church.

So, I told him how I speak in tongues and if I was going to be a youth pastor I couldn't leave the spirit out. He said that was fine that he wanted me to be myself and follow the Lord! So I accepted. Within three weeks we went from three youth to 30! Yes! When the kids at the high school learned that I was a youth pastor they wanted to go with me.

The 30 students who were going went every service! I had a little Chevy Chevette car and I would pack it out with like ten teenagers and my three children! We would cram everyone in there to go to church. They were so hungry for God.

I was in the process of planning a Youth Lock-in at the end of the school year and we were inviting the whole school. We handed out 1,000 flyers! This church only held 100 people. I invited Clarksville First Assembly of God youth group to come minister through dramas and singing. It was scheduled for a Friday night.

So, the Wednesday night before the actual Lock-in, I was giving a report to the church about Friday night's meeting. One of the elders of the church (There was only about 20 people who went to church there in older people). So, he said, "I don't like what you're doing to our church. There are more youth here than adults. I think you're putting the cart before the horse."

So, they gave me a warning and told me that they are all coming Friday night and if I get out of line once they are kicking me out. They said all of this in front of the 30 students.

All of a sudden one student raised their hand and the pastor let them talk and he said, "When I met this substitute teacher Mrs. Knight, I was into witchcraft and very deeply depressed. I heard her testify about Jesus and I gave my life to the Lord. Because of my change, the other seven people sitting next to me have become Christians too."

Then another girl stood up, "Yes, one night I was planning on killing myself the next day and I went to school believing this was my last day on Earth. Our teacher didn't show up and there is Mrs. Knight. She started telling the class about her life of abuse and how God saved her. I gave my life to the Lord in class and now I'm not depressed anymore! I thank God for Mrs. Knight."

Then one after another testified up to all 30. Then the pastor rebuked the elders who came against me and said, "OK, ya'll tell me who brings ten children to church in their little car with three kids in there as well? Who goes out of their way for souls?" So, they left the night that they was all coming Friday night with stipulations.

Friday night comes and it was a blow-out! 110 students from the high school came! The church was packed out! It was like 90% were not saved! 75 students got saved in one night! Almost all of them got baptized, etc. The pastor baptized students all night long!

When Clarksville First Assembly came in they did skits that had the whole place in tears. It was very dramatic and helped with the preaching. We had a lot of the students who testified Wednesday night stand up and tell their whole story to their friends at school. So many kids got delivered and healed that night. Well I only lasted two more weeks before the elders ran me off. They couldn't stand the spirit moving in the church.

The Loss of a Love

I met this guy after my divorce that was in our town. He was my age and had epilepsy. We fell for each other pretty hard and this is his story:

When he was about seven years old his dad was a Oneness Pentecostal Preacher. He got mad at him one day and hit him over the head with a 2x4. This caused him to have epilepsy. So he began having seizures. He got bitter when he became a teenager and rebelled against the church. So, by the time I met him he was 25 years old, living behind his parent's house and fighting to get on disability because he couldn't hold a job due to the seizures.

Well we would have long talks and I would tell him how God loves him and that he needed to forgive his dad. Well I ended up going back to ex-husband due to pressure from family and I had to leave him. My family hated him because of the different religion. (Not hated but disapproved). So, I went back to ex. It devastated the boyfriend.

Years later I was going through my contacts and called him. I told him I was coming to town the next morning and would love to see him. He got so excited and told me he wanted to tell me something the next day. He said he had great news! Something told me to call him that night about 11 p.m. but I didn't do it because his phone was same as his parents and I didn't want to wake him up.

So next morning when I arrived he didn't answer the door but he told me night before to just come on in. So, when I come in I heard the alarm going off. I walked in the living room and saw him in the dark sitting up on the couch. I thought he just wanted to surprise me so I said, "Hello! Good morning!" I went to turn the light switch on over his head and when I did I was so shocked! HE WAS DEAD! He had vomit all over him and his leg was stuck straight out with his hand out as well. He obviously had a seizure hours ago and froze in that position.

So I ran to his mom's house and banged on the door. I told her Wayne was in trouble that he was blue. She said, "Awe, he does that all the time it's ok." So, when she came out there she started screaming, "Nooooooooooo, No you can't leave me...no! I've got to call his dad!" So she ran to the house and called him. She said, "Honey, you need to come home, something's wrong with our son. He's not responding, come now." So she gets off phone and tells me to go be with him until the ambulance comes.

So I go back over to his house and I'm all alone with him but I felt him in the room with me. I felt him staring at me. I said, "Honey, I know you can hear me. I'm so sorry I didn't stay with you. I went back to my ex because I was pressured by my family. Please forgive me. I love you."

So, this guy had two children that were my kid's age and they loved me. They loved my kids too. They all had so much fun playing. He had one daughter and one son. He had full custody of them because the mom was out on drugs and was not in their life.

When the dad comes home he walked in and said, "Where's our son at?" She said, "Honey, he's gone, he's dead." When she said that, he dropped his lunch pail and fell to the floor screaming and crying, "No! God I'm so sorry! I'm so sorry! Please forgive me!" It was the saddest thing to watch.

Well the dad went to get the kids from school to tell them. When they come home they come running up to me screaming, "June! Daddy was going to ask you to marry him today! He loved you! We wanted you to be our momma!" We all were crying.

Well at the funeral I was standing by the casket looking at him and his mom came up to me and said, "June, I need to tell you something. The good news that he was going to tell you is that one week ago he came to church with his hair cut off, a suit on, and his earring out of his ear.

He walked right in to the front of the church and the pastor preached, 'Is your name written in the Lamb's Book of Life' and he walked to the altar and gave his life back to the Lord! He wanted to tell you that he made peace with God then he wanted to marry you! He also was granted his disability so he took all of us to Disneyworld last year." I stood there crying. I am so thankful though that he made peace with God and I praise God that I was instrumental in that.

Second Marriage

Well the ex-husband got jealous after a few months of me being with this guy so he came back and we remarried. I was tired of fighting my family. He said he was in counseling and wanted to go to church, etc. He went to church one time and abused the dog again and when I confronted him to ask him if he was going to counseling to talk about why he did that he said, "No. I got you now, I don't need counseling anymore."

So, I saw he wasn't changing so I divorced him.

Sugar Daddies Began – Easy Money

After the first divorce, the contractor that built our house was in his 70s. He was always attracted to me. He always flirted with me and told me how beautiful I was. So, after the divorce he knew I was so desperate for money.

Devil says, "How much do you need?" I said, "$1,200." He says, "Give me one hour and I will give it to you." So, after battling with the temptation for a long time and the pressures mounted, I took him up on it. This began easy money. In my worldly thinking I would rather get something out of the sex versus the men using me. They helped me take care of my family and I helped the needs they had as well. So, it worked out both ways. I was going to have sex with someone anyways so why not get paid for it.

Over the years this would be my crutch. When I got tight for money, I'd place an ad on Craigslist and meet another man. I would do anything to survive and take care of my children. When my children got older, I told them what I did and to this day it still bothers my daughter. I'm very ashamed of what I did, but nothing I can do about it now.

Going to College – Trying to Better Myself

Following that divorce I went to community college. I always regretted not graduating high school because I knew I was smart and not living up to my potential. So, I went to Nashville Tech and was studying Office Administration. I wanted to be a secretary. Well I got out of church and started partying and lost 90 lbs. I was sleeping around and loved all the attention I got from men. It was nice actually having men see the beauty in me, or so I thought. Truth be told, I opened the door to lust demons.

The Neighbor Devil

The neighbor across the street looked like he had been separated from his wife for at least six months when we started talking. I had him over for dinner one night and we slept together. He lied to me and his wife came after me. I told her that he told me he was divorced and I was honest with her. One day she had her family down the road plan an attack against me. I ended up having to fight that woman to defend myself. When I finished with her I had all my nails stuck in the top of her head (they were acrylic). I was hitting her and saying, "I told you I was sorry! I told you I was sorry!" I walked in the house and my boys who watched through the window said, "Wow mom, you did awesome! You slammed her over your back like a wrestler!" We laughed. I told them I only did that out of self-defense!

Hope of a Better Future

After that fiasco, my mom talked me into selling my house and moving in with her. It sounded nice, but ended up not being a great move. It wasn't all her fault because it was a combination of hoping my mother was telling the truth about helping us and tired of that neighborhood. However, that house went by my income and was perfect for me and the kids.

But, mom made it sound so appealing because she convinced me that she would help with the kids while I went to school, etc. First of all, she didn't approve of me going back to school. She thought I was too old for that and wasting my time.

Through much turmoil in the home, I knew I had to get my kids out of there! So, I had to quit school and go to work full-time to support the kids.

The Serial Tube-Tier

I met this man and was having a fling with him and he said, "I will marry you if you tie your tubes because I do not want any more children." So, I had the surgery and was laid up for six weeks recovering. When I recovered, he broke off engagement. Come to find out he did that to many women. He would propose then make them tie their tubes then leave them!

Third Marriage

After quitting college I went to work at Opryland Hotel, I met this other man. He was Puerto-Rican. He was the first other race I had ever dated. You could even hardly tell he was another race because he was white and beautiful. He had sparkling blue eyes with nice tan skin and he was 25 years-old. The only way you could tell was his course hair.

We ended up having a summer fling and got married. I went through a lot of rejection over him because of his race. My family disowned me, etc. I didn't care because I wanted him. He left me three weeks later for another woman. To top it off, she was a younger woman! This is after I moved out from my mothers and we got an apartment together. So now I'm stuck with this lease too. The judge would not let me get an annulment because we were married three weeks.

Fourth Marriage

Following this divorce, the ex-husband gets jealous again so he comes back wanting to work it out again. He said he wants his family back. I told him that I did too but I did not want it the way it was. He promised that he wanted to go to church, settle down, and live on his family's property in the country. He said it had always been a dream of his.

So. We go look at the land on Smiley Hollow Road. Next door to the land was his grandpa's house, on the other side was his aunt, and two doors down was his dad. Over the years the family had sold the 8 acres. Now it's for sale again and he wanted it.

He stood on the land and made a deal with God. He said, "God, if you will give my family back to me, this land, and a house to put on this land, then I will serve you the rest of my life." All of us were looking at him and we all prayed together. It was a special moment.

Then I saw him go to church with me and give his life to the Lord. It seemed so sincere. So we got married again. God gave him the land, the family and the biggest double-wide they make. It was nice! It was four bedrooms, three baths, two living rooms, etc. His family helped him put it in and set him up. It was a dream come true for all of us. He went to church one time. He didn't physically abuse anyone anymore, but it was all mental.

The Tornado in Smiley Hollow

When we married for the third time, we lived in a nice big modular home. It was the biggest they made. 2600 or 2100 square feet with four bedrooms, three baths, two living rooms, etc. Just gorgeous! We lived on almost eight (8) acres and it was the kid's dream. There was a creek behind our house and the kids would play in the creek all day long. Behind the creek was a steep mountain and they didn't care. They would climb that mountain like little explorers and bring different snakes home to show momma, lol. I had a big dinner bell and I'd either ring it or say, "Kids dinner is ready...come home."

So one day this tornado was coming down our holler. In our holler it was in between two mountains. So, if the tornado was coming, we would be plowed down! It was hailing outside, raining so hard and the winds were shaking the house. Daddy was at work so me and the kids hid in the closet in me and their dad's room. We all held on to each other and we prayed:

We could hear it on our street like a train running through the house. The house shook violently. We kept praying and asking God to put angels around our house and to protect us.

After the tornado left, we walked outside and the tornado had hit every house on the street but ours! It tore the roof off some of the other ones too. God protected us!

Rocky, the Famous Dog of Smiley Hollow

Grandpa lived two doors down from us on Smiley Hollow Road. Being that we lived in the country and in the holler, it was like living in our own world because we didn't see much traffic and we experienced nature all the time. We saw deer and all kinds of animals.

Well grandpa owned a dog named Rocky. Rocky was a big dog kind of like a German Shepherd, Rottweiler, etc. I don't know exactly what kind of dog but he was known in the neighborhood as the family mutt.

Rocky was famous because he would roam the street and let every family feed him. He was a very friendly dog and good with the children. The children in our neighbor were in love with him.

The kids would act like they're drowning in the creek and he would jump in and pull them out. He walked with them in the woods and protected them. They felt safe with him.

He lived to a good 'old age.

Jesus Came to See Brock 2nd Time

When Brock was ten (10) years old we were attending Faith Covenant Church in Springfield, TN. We had an evangelist visit one night (don't remember who) and at the alter call he prayed for Brock. When he touched Brock, he fell on the floor (slain in the spirit). He was on the floor about an hour.

I knew Brock was having an experience with God because he was weeping and speaking in tongues. As a mom we know these things in the spirit.

On the way home he said, "Mom, Jesus came to see me tonight and this time I heard what he said." I eagerly asked, "What did he say Brock?"

Brock said, "He told me that he's called me to preach to the nations momma!"

I started weeping. I was saying, hallelujah. How wonderful for God to call my son! No one in my family had ever been called to preach before. I was rejoicing...until we got home and he told his dad.

His dad told him to go get a belt. He went to get the belt and handed it to his dad. His dad whipped him and with every lash he would say;

NO SON OF MINE IS GOING TO BE A LOW-DOWN, NO-GOOD-FOR-NOTHIN' LAZY PREACHER! DON'T BE A WUSS; A SISSY!

He whipped him every day for six weeks! He would call him names and proclaim he WILL NOT BE A PREACHER!

In the meantime while Brock is getting whipped for no reason...the anointing increased in Brock's life. During this time the following things happened:

He would pray for his classmates at school and they got saved, healed and delivered. It would be in the classrooms, on the playground, or anywhere.

He cast demons out of a mean bully on the school bus. The bus driver got mad at this bully and made him sit with the preacher-kid up front. He tried to bully Brock and he said, "Satan, get thee behind me and leave this boy!" That boy got delivered and became a different kid!

Other miracles, signs and wonders but I can't remember them all.

I think in his father's eyes he remembers Brock coming home from school talking about how kids persecuted him and called him names like sissy and wuss. So, he told him he didn't want him doing that!

We didn't stay married too long after all this. Ironically enough, Brock grew up to preach his grandpa's funeral (his dad's dad). Me and Brock was at his grandpa's bedside and prayed salvation with him before he took his last breath. We were there when Jesus took him home.

I wonder what his dad thought as he sat there listening to his son preach his father's funeral. I know that since the funeral his dad hates me more.

I pray for him. He was my first love. :) Also, Brock and his dad made peace and are very close now. His dad remarried and is very happy now. :)

P.S. Grandpa was like a dad to me. I visited him even after the divorce until the day he died. I always kept the kids in contact with him over the years. So, on his deathbed I told him how much I love him and thanked him for always loving me. I'm happy knowing he's with Jesus!

Brock and the Letter to God

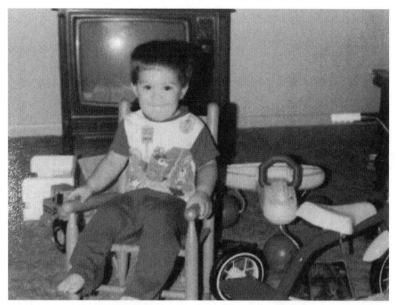

I remember days where Brock and Andrew would be praying in their room and stomping on the devil. They would say, "Devil, leave me alone, leave my family alone", etc. We took our prayers seriously with God.

One night in our big country trailer, this storm came. It was shaking the trailer and the rain was coming down so hard. Me and the kids were praying for God to protect our home. Next thing you know Brock walked up to me, "Mom, I need you to open the front door I need to give this to God." I looked down and it was a piece of paper and a note written on it. I said, "Can't we just pray about it?"

He said, "No, I need him to take this one to Heaven."

So, I opened the front door and the wind about blew the door off the hinges. Brock said, "Take it Lord." He threw the letter out in the storm and we both watched as it blew up in the air like the Lord was receiving it. We shut the door and Brock looked very happy knowing God accepted his letter. The storm stopped about five minutes later.

I never found out what was on that letter.

Brock's Bully at School

Brock was at Greenbrier Middle School and a neighbor down the road constantly harassed him and picked on him in school. This boy was labeled a child with special-needs.

One day Brock came home and said that he was at the water fountain and this boy walked up behind him and slammed his head down on the water fountain and busted his lip. I asked him if he told on the boy and he said yes that he told the teacher. A couple of days later he said the boy walked up behind him in class and pulled his hair. He told again.

Next incident the boy walked by him and slammed the locker door on his fingers. Per our instructions, he went to the principal this time. The principal told him there wasn't anything he could do because it was on the boy's school

assessment that he had violence disorder and all kinds of other disorders.

The principle declared that his hands were tied with the State of TN. In other words, if you are legally declared mean and abusive to other people and you act out on that at school with normal children, the other children just have to suffer because now everyone has to work around all that. Well, that's what happened.

After Brock putting up with that time and time again and him honoring our request by going to the teachers, principal, etc., and nothing being done, his dad just told him one day, "Son, it looks like you're just going to have to fight back. You're going to have to defend yourself against this bully." Now, I wouldn't have advised that…but that is what his father advised him.

So, Brock goes to school the next day and the student takes a milk carton full of milk and slams it down in front of Brock and splashes milk all over him and laughs while he's mocking Brock. Brock comes home that night and informs his parents that he is suspended from school because when the student did that, Brock lost it and jumped across the table and threw the boy on the ground and beat him up. The teachers didn't stop him.

So, after Brock was finished, the principal suspended him for three days.

The next day we went to the school and talked to the principal to defend Brock. Following that incident, the boy never touched Brock again and ended up becoming really good friends with Brock.

The Salty Green Beans

As a mother I've always believed in the big dinners and the family eating together at the dinner table. I believe this is the breakdown of the American Family; when we got away from the family eating together. I grew up watching the Walton's and I admired their family-togetherness.

When I cooked dinners for my family it consisted of big southern meals. A big southern meal is like fried chicken, mashed potatoes, macaroni and cheese, green beans cooked in hog jowl, and cornbread cooked in the iron skillet. Also, in the south you cannot have dinner without sweet tea!

I make world-famous sweet tea! I'm known world-wide, lol. (Based upon Bible College students).

Anyways, this one country day I made a big dinner as such mentioned above. At this time I was married to the kid's dad and they were all under the age of twelve years-old.

At this meal their dad came home from work and the table was full of home-cooked food and we all sat down to eat. Each person loaded their plates and as they're eating their dad remarks, "Man these beans are salty." I said, "No they're not just eat" LOL. Then one kid, then another, until everyone at the table is spitting the beans out of their mouth.

I WAS INSULTED! How dare them! LOL

Then their dad says, "Give some to the dog and see if he thinks it's too salty." So the kids put some in the dog's bowl and all eyes are on this dog's reaction...He takes ONE bite and spits it all out and runs howling to his water bowl! OMG we laughed so hard! We couldn't even hardly finish eating for laughing about the salty green beans. :)

The Final Divorce with Kid's Dad

We were married three years this time and we tried so hard to make it work. He hated me being a Christian and going to church with the kids. When we would go he was mean. When we wouldn't go we had peace in the home. For a while we didn't go. It was a constant battle.

We have good memories in this house as well as bad. One of the main reasons I believe that led to the divorce was his family on the street. He allowed them to persecute me severely. I started taking my mother-in-law's daughter who was a drug-addict and prostitute to church. She got delivered. When my mother-in-law found out she called me every day and would say, "You better leave my F'in daughter alone! Don't take her to that F'in Pentecostal Church!" She was Baptist and hated me being Pentecostal. So I told my husband to please call his dad and make her stop and he said, "Well you shouldn't be going to that type of church!"

So this went on for about six months I guess. Well in the meantime I was praying over her daughter's house one day and the Holy Spirit would show me things about their family and I'd cast all that off. Well, she didn't believe any of it until her kids got home from school and confessed to the sins that the Holy Spirit had revealed. So, here they come to my doorstep that night while I was cooking dinner. They were crying and said they want the Holy Ghost too.

So I prayed for all three of them and they got filled with the Holy Ghost. God really changed this family. The wife got back with her husband and God was healing the whole family.

In the meantime the mother was getting madder. One day I was having a prayer meeting at the daughter's apartment with about 12 other ladies from the apartment complex. I just told those ladies that I saw angels in the room. They were as tall as the complex and had flaming swords in their hands. Well I was sitting on the floor in front of the front door and all the other ladies were sitting around the room. All of a sudden the front door slammed open! It was my mother-in-law full of rage!

She said, "I thought I told you to stay away from my daughter!" She came straight towards me and reared her fist back to punch me in the nose when she got about 10 inches something stopped her fist mid-air and she was fighting this force! Her eyes got wide as saucers and she ran out of the room in terror! She slammed the door behind her.

The other women in the room…their mouths were dropped to the floor. I told them that angels were in the room.

Well sad thing is that the mother-in-law got her Baptist pastor to come see her after that and convince her that I was of the devil. The girl went back out on the streets into prostitution and drugs. I received a phone call one day from my mother-in-law, "I'd rather see her out there than in a Pentecostal church!"

Another incident that comes to mind is when the family got together and called the police on our dog and lied saying he bit a little girl that lived at the house next door. They didn't even have a little girl. They lied. So, the police come in our yard and shot our dog for no reason in front of Brock. It was like a horror scene. His eye was hanging out and blood was going everywhere and he was trying to save us as he was dying.

The family sat in the driveway laughing at our screaming and horror of our family dog that was born under our house on Christmas Eve was dying. We ended up saving the dog but I was so mad at my husband. I told him if he would have stopped his family from harassing me years ago this would not have happened. He ended up having to shoot that dog later because he went crazy from the shrapnel in his head.

Well, one day he said, "I'm going to take that dog to the creek and set him on fire and burn him to death." I looked at him and I thought, "Do I want my children growing up and talking like that in front of their kids? Do I want them treating their wives like he treats us?" So we mutually divorced that time. I was about to turn 30 and we just knew it was over.

The Dad I Never Knew

I never really knew my dad. The only memories I have of him growing up is bad memories. He was mean, alcoholic, abusive, and had caused mom to have four miscarriages. I did not have a good impression of what a father was.

They divorced when I was five, then the next time I saw him as a child was not a good experience either.

So, the only things I did know about him is that he was an aspiring country music singer. They moved to Nashville to get in the singing business. He was very good at singing and playing the guitar. I take that back about only having bad memories. I just remembered a good memory. I remember he used to tell us stories about this character named "Snookums". Snookums always got in trouble at school for having poop in his pants and flies following him everywhere. We would laugh so hard. I do remember Snookums stories.

After I got married and went through the hell of that abuse and realized I married someone just like my father, it was a sad realization.

Of course, we all know that it's not flesh and blood we fight. It's the demons operating through these people that came at me. I'm not blaming the people (husband or dad). It's the demons that tried to take us out.

Anyways, the good news is that the last 10 years of his life he gave his life to the Lord and stopped drinking! Yes! God delivered him of alcoholism! He was not that old man anymore.

However, when I did see him during that time at family reunions, he was so out of his mind due to the alcohol that he could not communicate right with us. Like, he couldn't talk about real things. He was very superficial. I believe it was due to the alcohol over the years.

So, at his funeral, I was more grieved at who I didn't know than him. Now, to my older brothers it was a different experience because they got to know him better than I did and on a different level.

I am currently working on building relationships with his side of the family. We are getting closer and I'm very thankful for God redeeming and restoring the time.

This is my last picture with my dad, RIP Clinton B. Carpenter – 01/12/00

Sex with the Devil

Right after the divorce me and the kids moved into an apartment in Greenbrier. The kids were heavily into their sports so I wanted to stay in their town. I was going to church and on fire for God. However, I still flirted with guys online. So one day I met this cute guy who invited me over for dinner. He lived about an hour away. So, I went and it was at night.

He was very good-looking and he seduced me. It was very erotic, I can't explain it. He didn't rape me but I almost couldn't control myself with him. We began to have sex and it was the weirdest sex I ever experienced. Remember when I wrote how when the devil came in the room when I was on the Ouija board and it became ice-cold in the room? Well, that's what happened with this man. It was ice-cold. It was very eerie and just felt wrong.

When we were finished I went into the bathroom and he had his class ring sitting on the counter. I looked at this ring and something told me, "Steal his ring." I shook that thought off and I thought, "Where did that come from?" So, I left there feeling so ashamed.

I knew all the goodness that was in me left. I felt like my Christianity just got sucked right out of me. So, I'm feeling all dirty and I arrive at a gas station to get me something to drink. It's about 1 a.m.

I had some cheerleading money in my purse in a pouch where we had done fund-raising. I knew it was about $100. When I was looking for the money in my wallet it was all gone, including the change in my zipper. Then I looked for that pouch of money and it was gone too! I was searching frantically! This fear came over me like, "Oh no, he stole your cheerleader's money!"

Next thing you know a man is standing in my window and he said, "Ma'am, it's not in there." I said, "Yes it is sir, I'm sure I just can't find it." So, I look down to find it and looked back up and he was gone. He disappeared! I dropped my hands and I knew it was an angel. I knew then that God had caught me and knew what I did. I was so ashamed. I just sat there crying telling God how sorry I was.

I kept calling that guy and he wouldn't answer the phone. So, I even went back to his apartment and was banging on his door and he wouldn't answer the door. I was devastated! I cried myself to sleep.

The next morning I called my mom and confessed. I asked her to please pray for me because I slept with the devil. She prayed with me and asked God to restore the money unto me. The devil had to pay back what he stole! So, that night the guy sent me a message on AOL (that's where we met), and told me I had left the money and for me to come get it. I got it that night but he did not restore the money out of my wallet.

I was happy to even get my cheer money back!

Needless to say, it took a long time to recover from opening the door to the devil like that!

My Ishmael – Devil With a Gay Suit On

Soon after that I met another man online. He was in Las Vegas Nevada and seemed perfect for me. He was tall, dark, and handsome. He was a Christian and had a personality like me. He was very outgoing and it just seemed perfect.

At this point in my life it seemed like God was bringing full restoration to my life. He gave my son back who was living with his dad for a year, gave me a local job driving a school bus in the same area as my church (Springfield), and a new boyfriend. Once the guy (Larry) asked me to marry him, the Lord blessed us with a home! It was beautiful! It was a log house, two-story, in the country, paved driveway and a 2-car garage.

However, I knew I couldn't pay for it without being married so I truly trusted this guy's word. It was like everything was being restored all the way around. I was so happy.

He flew in to visit me and it was perfect! I took him to meet my cheerleading commissioners and they loved him, my family loved him, etc. He loved the house too! My kids loved him too. Well, after he left the cheerleading cities (there was 13 total) said they would pay for the wedding if we did a cheerleading wedding. They suggested we could get married at competition and allow the girls to be in the wedding too. So, this became the plans for this massive wedding:

500 cheerleaders total from 10 different cities and they were going to line up from one end of the arena to the other and hold their pom-poms up in the

air to show unity in cheerleading and I was going to walk underneath them to the platform.

The Tennessee Titans Football Team Cheerleaders were the judges that year so they were going to be in the wedding on the platform like bridesmaids.

The football league was going to be on the groom's side. The football commissioners would be with him.

MTJLCA Cheer Commissioners would be on my side.

All the cities were paying for it.

News Channel 5 was going to be there to feature the unusual cheerleading unity wedding. All the communities would be there.

So, needless to say I was so excited about this big wedding. I started driving a school bus in this new county and within one month everything fell apart and my world collapsed.

The School Bus Disaster

As I began driving for this new county, the training is severely lacking compared to Nashville. I did not have route sheets to tell me where to pick up the children and I was told to listen to the students. In Nashville they gave each driver route sheets to guide them on the route. This school system taught me to listen to the children's guidance.

So, one day these children told me the wrong spot to drop off these two little kids. One was in Kindergarten and the other one was in 1st Grade. They got off the bus in the beginning of the route with like ten other children. I watched them in my side mirror walk towards a house.

Well that night I got a phone call from my dispatcher and he said, "Why did you drop off those children at the wrong spot?" After I realized who he was talking about I replied, "I don't have route sheets to tell me like they did when I worked in Nashville and since your company tells me to just drop them off where other students tell me that's what I did." So, he told me that I was in big trouble.

So next day I was substitute teaching and the Director of Transportation come and pulled me out of class and sent me home. He told me that I had to be on suspension without pay until further investigation.

71

I then had to go to a meeting where I had to explain what happened at the School Board office.

When I worked in Nashville for three years they had a union and whenever you were accused of something you had representation.

This school system didn't have any representative for me. So, the next day when I had this meeting I heard that the bus drivers were having a meeting to discuss trying to bring in a union like Nashville had. Well, I went to the meeting and they fired me! Not only did they fire me, but they told me that the mother of the children was pressing charges against me for Child Neglect. I was looking at two years prison sentence. I told them that they are trying to produce an escape goat for a system that sets up drivers for failure. I had only been with the system for three weeks. This was my first day on that route. I didn't know what I was doing. So, when I knew they fired me, I knew I lost my house.

Back to the Story of The Ishmael

Right after that, it was two weeks before competition and the wedding and my fiancé' called and said that he is not marrying me because he went back to his ex-wife who left him for another woman. He left me for a lesbian. So, I was getting hit on every side.

Then I had to call the commissioners and not only tell them the wedding was off, but that they fired me. Then it went on the news! The woman went public and lied about me. She told the world that I dropped the kids off at the end of my route that no one else was on the bus that I just pointed to them and yelled at them and said, "Get off my bus now and walk down this highway alone!" I mean totally lied!

So here I was on national television, falsely accused, wedding cancelled, lost my job, and it's dead of winter. Here I am with this expensive house, heating/air went out so now I have no heat, and publicly humiliated before I stand before thousands as Emcee of this event, etc. My world just absolutely got crushed!

Competition rolls around and God gave me the strength to make it through the day! We had a huge glitch happen at the end of the day because the judges cheated and it cost a city some trophies so that city bombarded the stage and was cussing me out. So, I had to calm that fire and ended up resigning over that and everything else happening!

So, now competition's over, money's gone, humiliation is at all-time high, and now they call and say they're going to arrest me. So, I drove to the police station, spent my last $800 I had saved for the house note to get out of jail. I had to get a public lawyer and it was just horrible.

I then started getting eviction notices because the house wasn't being paid and I was totally desperate to provide a roof for my kids.

So, I meet someone online again. He had a home in Clarksville and we got married a few weeks later. I gave up my house and moved in to his and remodeled his from top to bottom.

Six months later the courts dropped the charges and I asked them, "Why did you wait so long to drop the charges?" They said, "We had to wait for the news media to die down." It was all to please the media! In the meantime my name is ruined and my life!

I realize now how God wanted me to lean on Him instead of a man, but because I was so codependent, I had to have help.

Fifth Marriage

We ended up being married a year and a half and it was miserable. He was 19 years older than me and we had nothing in common. I married him for the wrong reason and I met him for lunch one day after a year and a half and said, "Well, you're obviously not going to have sex with me so since you're making that choice I'm giving you a choice. I'm a woman with needs so I can either get a boyfriend to fulfill that need and we stay married or we can get a divorce, what do you think we should do?" He said, "Get a boyfriend." He was serious too.

Well I thought about it for a week considering my past, but after talking to his daughter who told me he wouldn't have sex with her mother either, which is why she left him for another man then he turned around and told the church that his wife left him. So, I told him a week later that I can't cheat on him and that I was not giving him an excuse to lie about me.

I wanted a divorce." I told him all he had to do was give me $1,000 to get a place and he could have the house. He refused.

So, one night he comes downstairs to my room and gets mad because I have worship music playing low. He walked over and turned my music off. So, I got up and walked over there and turned it back up. Then he assaulted me. He slammed me up against the desk and was trying to punch my computer and stuff, so we end up fighting. I reach up to the phone and dial 911. I told them my husband was assaulting and he walks in the garage and shuts off the lights to the house so my phone dies.

The kids are upstairs asleep so I run upstairs and the phone rings. It's 911 again. They're asking why the phone got disconnected and I told them my husband had flipped out because I'm wanting a divorce and the police arrived. Do you know that man took his fingers and scratched himself to bleeding and told the police I did that! So, they took us both to jail!

I Went to Jail – Over a Man!

Being that I've never been in jail, this was a scary experience! I walked in the cell with the other 20 or so women and this big butchy-type of woman walked up to me and said, "When you get your food you better give it to me." I looked at her like I could punch her in the face and I said, "Woman, you don't want to mess with me. I've been fighting with my husband all night and I'm still pretty mad. If I have food left I will give it to you." I did give her most of it because the food was horrible!

I had to stay in jail for 16 hours and I heard the guards talking while I was going to see the magistrate and they were saying how the women rape one another, etc. They were trying to scare me.

Well, I get before the judge and the husband shows her the scratches and she looks at me all mad like I did it and I said, "Your honor, please look at my fingernails and tell me how I could do that and look at his. I bite my nails so I have no nails. He did that on purpose because he's mad that I want a divorce." Then I began to tell her how he wouldn't have sex with me and I've tried counseling and everything and how he wanted me to get a boyfriend, etc. So then when she saw the truth this was her ruling, "Sir, you could have gotten the house for only $1,000 if you would have let her go.

Because you refused to let her go and her three children, you will need to move out. I'm going to allow the wife and three children to stay in the house and you have to pay for it as long as she's living there.

You will pay all bills too until this divorce is final!" She hung him!

He moved out and I could have stayed there and milked that for all it's worth. However, a week later the Lord told me to give him his house back.

I called him and gave the house back. Then when we went to divorce the Lord told me to give him whatever he wanted. Man, he started out saying, "I want the sectional." I reluctantly agreed. Then it was him wanting everything! Even the dog! I left there with nothing but my kids. However, I obeyed God! All the charges were dropped against one another as well.

Athletic Family Genes

The children didn't really have a chance at not being an athlete because both of their parents were very athletic. I was a dancer and cheerleader and their dad was the all-state football player. As soon as my oldest son turned five years-old, I had the children in sports. The boys played football and baseball and Meagan did cheerleading and gymnastics. The boys were not as good at basketball as Meagan was not so good at softball. However, they were all beasts at their sports.

The boys often made all-stars and Meagan and I won championships. We played the card game SPOONS and had the funnest time because we were all

very competitive. It is in our genes to be the best at everything we do.

No matter what circumstances my family faced, whether I was single again, or with someone, it never interrupted the children's games or lifestyle of sports. Whatever city we lived in, that is the first thing I would do is sign them up for sports.

I believe this had a huge play in why the children turned out as great as they have in spite of their past. Sports kept them with friends and an active life and a great distraction.

They all played right through high school. The boys heard stories growing up about their dad and their uncle being just one year apart and the school calling them the Knight Brothers and how everyone feared them. So, when the boys got in high school they were honored to carry on that tradition.

Jesus Comes to See Brock 3rd Time

 We were at a revival at First Assembly of God and they all knew Brock's giftings so we were at the altar and all of a sudden I saw Brock walk up on the platform. I thought, "Oh no, pastor doesn't like anyone up there." But no one said anything. Then for the next hour, you just saw Brock walking back and forth praying in tongues and you knew he was in the throne room. It was very powerful and intimate.

So, on the way home he said, "Momma, Jesus came to see me again." I started to catch on that it was every five years! So I said, "What did He say this time?" Brock replied, "He told me to give up football now and start preaching now!" My heart sank because I knew what that meant. Brock was a sophomore in high school and he was already the captain of the football team and already had scouts looking at him. I was like, "Oh no." He said,

"Yes, I know mom so please pray for me."

So, right after that I go to Florida to help my cousin and I'm praying and the Holy Spirit says, "When you get back home Brock is going to come up to you and say that he is going to get back on the football team and how they are going to go to State, etc., and this is what I want you to tell him. Tell him that he DOES have to quit football and begin preaching now."

So, I get back home and as soon as I pull up he comes running out to the car screaming, "Mom! I'm back on the football team. They need me to go to State, etc." He said everything Holy Spirit said he would. So I let him finish then I said, "Brock, the Holy Spirit told me that you would say that in Florida so this is what He says, and I told him. He about cried.

He kept trying to convince me why he should and I wouldn't budge. I told him we must obey God no matter what.

He said, "Momma, just take me to the church and let me pray for three hours and I'll know. My head is just so confused right now!

76

So, I picked him up three hours later and you could tell he was in the presence of the Lord. He said, "Mom, you were right. I have a very clear head now. Thank you! Just pray for me because I'm under so much persecution!

Because of that decision, he went through hell for a couple of years but he ended up winning almost his whole high school to Christ!

Columbine Called

One day Brock come home from school and said that this group was at the school today from Columbine where that girl got killed for Jesus by a classmate. It was her aunt and uncle. Brock began to explain that the whole school was assembled in the gymnasium and they were talking about how she made a stand for Christ and got shot in the head. Well the Holy Spirit told Brock to go to them and ask for the microphone and they just handed it to him. He began preaching and about 200 kids got saved, filled with the Holy Ghost and healed that day! They were at the altar crying and everything!

So, that night that aunt and uncle called me to tell me what a special boy I had. They said that they were in Colorado and got an email about a special boy in Clarksville, TN. They didn't know his name but that people get healed through him, etc. So, they spoke in all the other schools but this one and it opened up at the last minute before they got on the plane to go back to Colorado.

So, when they saw Brock walk up there, that's why they handed him the microphone because they already knew about him. They wanted him to travel with them to win high schools for Jesus. Brock told them he would pray about it.

He ends up telling them that he could not do it because God called him to Clarksville. So, he ended up winning his school for Christ. They loved him so much that at the senior prom, they voted him King and gave him a standing ovation for a while saying, "Thank you, thank you, thank you!" If you read his annual it's like reading an obituary thanking him for all the healings and salvations, etc.

Brock at his Tuesday night Youth meetings while he was in high school.

PRESIDENT OF A LOCAL STEELWORKER'S UNION

After the last fiasco of driving a school bus in Springfield and losing everything I had over a false accusation and no union to represent me, I was forced to go back to work driving a bus again in another city. I was divorcing the 5th husband so I got a job in Clarksville to drive again. I tried so hard to lay low so they wouldn't find out that I was the one on TV being accused of dropping off those two children in Springfield a few years before. I just minded my own business and took care of my children.

Well I was a good bus driver so at the end of that first year they made me like Bus Driver of the Year. That isn't what it was called but it meant the same. Here's how I found out:

One morning I was in a hurry so I threw my hair up in a ponytail, no makeup and a t-shirt. My normal attire was very dressy and with makeup on. So this one morning it was right before Christmas break and I had fun stuff I did with my elementary kids all the time. I'd have the microphone in my hand and when I rode down a street I'd say, "And now, look to the left children and you will see Rudolph leading the sleigh! Now let's sing, Rudolph the Red Nosed Reindeer!" Or I would say stuff like, "Oh no, look at the big Santa Clause on the right, he got in a fight and fell over!" LOL. I would just say funny stuff and make the kids laugh.

So this morning we had to wait 10 minutes for school to open their doors so we were on the bus singing Christmas carols. Sometimes I read the children books or told them funny stories. This morning was my worst nightmare.

This man knocks on my door and I opened it. He said, "Ma'am, I'm with the Leaf Chronicle. Your school system voted you like bus driver of the year and we need to interview you." I was like, "NOOOOOOOOOOOOOO NOT THE WAY I'M DRESSED PLEASE." LOL. Well he interviewed me and some children and took a picture of us as a group. He said the principal of that school nominated me because I taught the children on the bus while we waited and sang with them, etc.

Well the school system didn't know that at the same time they were doing that, the bus drivers were calling a meeting to determine if they wanted a bus driver's union like Nashville had. They knew I drove in Nashville for three years, but they didn't know me as much because I laid low for that year.

The morning of the meeting the Lord woke me up and told me, "Go to them and ask them if you can pray for the meeting." So I did. They said, "Man, we've been looking for someone, yes!" So, when the Nashville drivers came in and saw me, they went crazy. They loved me in Nashville so it was great for the Clarksville drivers to see the favor. At least I was able to tell them that the Springfield incident was a false accusation and they said they already knew it was and how bad that city needed a union. I told them that after I left the meeting in Springfield when they fired me, I walked into their meeting to tell them THIS IS WHY YOU NEED A UNION. I had no one to fight for me and they were defending their self. They were in the wrong for not having route sheets but they blamed me and I was the escape goat.

Anyway, when it comes time to pray, the anointing was all over it. I was praying because I was a person that lost it all without union protection so I prayed the fire down. I said, "I come against Pharaoh moving against our drivers! I command the truth to be made known and for justice to happen through God!" They gave me a standing ovation when I finished! They didn't know WHY I had that fire.

When they saw the passion they asked me to be on their union board. I gladly accepted. A couple of weeks later the system gave me that award and my picture was on the front page of the paper on Christmas Eve and it was called, "Wheels on the Bus Go Round and Round". The bus drivers were shocked at how I looked in the paper because I was bummed out and not dressed up like usual. I was like, "Yeah, the one day I dressed like that they caught me" LOL. We all laughed.

So, the new year rolls around and I start going to the board meetings and bringing it to the light about what was going on behind closed doors to the bus drivers. I was telling the stories of bus drivers who were in the room to the School Board Members. There were about 200 bus drivers in there. We had like 330 out of 333 bus drivers in the union. It was just a few off. This is how bad that system was treating their drivers. They would chew them out all the time on the radio like children in front of the principals, school board members, etc. I would get so mad just listening to them but I was determined to stay out of it. Then one day they disciplined a driver on the radio. It was crazy. One time a driver fell down in between the two routes and broke her arm and called in to dispatch and told them that she needed to go to the hospital and they told her that she had to drive the next route then they would send someone. She had to drive in all that pain with one arm.

This one driver was notified one night that their brother died and they called in and they would not let them have off the three days. Another driver had a head-on collision with a car and killed two people. She was coming over a hill and there was a car dead-parked in the road on her side so she swerved to other side and hit a truck head-on. I may be off on the details a little but that's the gist of it. The point is that she killed two people and was a nervous wreck. They kept her in the office without offering her food or water all morning then made her drive that afternoon after she told them she could not do it. It was stuff like this. They were ruthless.

So, as I was revealing these things the drivers would picket outside the board room, we was on the news and in the papers all the time so we were putting the pressure on the school system to relieve the drivers. Most drivers worked many more hours a day than they got paid, etc. They definitely needed a union.

A couple months later after we formed we had elections. This guy won president and I was running for Vice President against a woman that was driving like 20 years. The only reason I won it is because I came out with my story. I told them how I can fight for them because I have nothing to lose. I know what it's like to lose it all on false accusations. So, I beat that woman. At first I got along great with that man and we made a great team until the school system got to him with money.

They called us in a meeting and asked us to come on "their side" and they will give us promotions and money to help them because the drivers respected us. I immediately turned it down because I knew they were not going to back down and I said, "No. We're not budging. We want a union and we want everything we're asking for." Well the president folded. He entertained the idea. I told them that when they talk to us they're not talking to just two people; they're talking to 330 other people who need fair pay, etc. So, when we left that meeting I asked that guy why he would even consider turning on the union, etc.

Well, he ended up turning and he would tell the director what I was going to say in my upcoming speeches and she would address those issues first before I spoke. I knew we had a mole in the camp. I knew it was him too.

Well come to find out, it was suspected that he was texting her inside information. Most drivers felt it was true when soon after they promoted him and he's still there today working in the office.

Well the school board director come off the platform one time when I was speaking because she was so mad at what I revealed. She said, "You don't tell people what you and I discuss behind closed doors." I said, "You're not talking to me, you're talking to 330 other drivers. This is not about me and you." So she got mad and stomped off.

The drivers suspected that our president had turned on us so we had an emergency meeting and they voted him out. At the elections they voted me in as president. I put even more heat on the school board director.

Well, she came after me but couldn't find anything on me. She had people follow me and everything. However, I had a perfect driving record and I was a good driver so she couldn't get me there.

Well, one day the principal at my elementary school died. The kids just loved her. On that Sunday, the day of her funeral, the Lord told me at church, "Go pick up kids on your route and offer to take them to her funeral." Man, when I went to their homes most of the mothers cried. One of them said, "I just prayed and asked God to send someone to take my daughter! I had a car accident this summer and I can't drive and she loves her so!" I ended up loading my van down with about 11 children in an 8-passenger van. So a couple of them I just double-buckled.

We arrive at the funeral and the principal's family was so blessed to see the group of children and the principal's brother pulled me aside and thanked me so much!

Well the director was at the funeral along with most other people in the county and they saw me with all these kids. Remember, this is on a Sunday in my own car and permission from their parents. So, I took the children home.

Two days later they call me on the radio and told me to go to the school board office that night at 5:00 p.m. for a meeting. At this meeting they asked me "Why did you take children to a funeral to see a dead body?" He said it very sarcastically and mean. I replied, "Because God told me to." He laughed and wrote it on his yellow pad all the way across it, "God told her to!" Then he told me I broke their school board policy. I inquired as to which one because I knew them all. He said, "We don't have one yet, but we will make one. You are going to pay big time for doing this! You are not allowed to drive those kids anywhere in any vehicle after school bus routes."

I said, "I drive those children to church on our church bus. Are you saying I can't do that either?" He said, "Yes, nowhere."

So I went and told the parents what they were trying to do and they called News Channel 5. We had a press conference on the grounds of the school system and I was being interviewed and the reporter asked me, "Does it bother you that the school board director is standing behind this camera staring at you while you're being interviewed?" I said, "No because I know she wants to fire me and she's just looking for an excuse."

The school system ended up suspending me for three weeks without pay to punish me. The bus drivers were so mad that they chipped in and paid my salary to help me. It stayed in the news and the picketing was hot every day! The community was on my side and when I would go places they would say, "Hey, you're that girl on TV, we're paying for your food, etc."

It ends up that the school board director made an announcement that she's retiring. I was so happy and so were the bus drivers.

However, politics began to play out with my vice president and the union rep. They started meeting on the side and ended up having an affair. They kinds of pushed me out so she could become president. It was fine with me because I had gotten everything I fought for.

The school system buckled and gave the drivers the hours they needed, the pay, insurance, better treatment, etc. They didn't get the union, but they did get better treatment.

The school board director when she found out I was retiring as president suddenly withdrew her notice to quit. She finally left that next year. Although I fought hard to get the drivers their due rights, I went through a lot of hell to get it too. To this day if any of my possible employers call them they have lied to some of them. One time they told another school system that I took the kids to that funeral in my bus! The good thing is that none of my other employers ever listened to them and I drove in many more counties after that!

THE UNIDENTIFIED CALL

After my fifth divorce, we were in the process of buying a house and we thought we had it secured so we all moved in. It was a beautiful home, very quaint, three bedroom, two full baths, nice backyard with woods behind it, etc.

It was in a brand new subdivision so we were able to build it from scratch and pick all the colors. We were very excited to have a home of our own again. Remember the last one we had we lost it due to that crazy bus incident.

So, we pick all the colors, cabinets, flooring and everything down to the knobs. We move in like we're the Beverly Hillbillies! LOL. We move in and my daughter is in her own room and the boys shared a room. We were like two miles from their high school and middle school and I was driving that route on my school bus. How nice was it to go out to the driveway every morning, start the bus, sit outside and drink my coffee waiting to get started.

My kids were able to ride my bus as well. One funny story:

The first morning on my route at the beginning of the year I asked my children, "What can I say to the children as they get on the bus to let them know I'm a cool bus driver?" Andrew says, "Just say, Yo Yo Yo, Wuz up my schnizzel my nizzel?" So, at the various stops I would say that as they got on the bus. They were mostly African-American and they just all looked at me funny.

So, I continued to do that periodically trying to be funny the first couple of months, but after the kids fell in love with me and we built a relationship I grabbed the microphone and said that and one of the high schoolers in the back said, "Ms. June, don't you know what you're saying when you say that?" I said, "No, what am I saying?" They said, "You're calling us all niggers!"

83

I said, "What? OMG, my son told me to say that and I thought ya'll would think I'm cool." They laughed and said, "Which son?" (They knew both of my sons very well). I told them. Well Andrew came home from school that night and said, "Momma, what did you tell the kids on the bus?" I told him. He replied, "Mom, they harassed me about it all day at school." I said, "Well you shouldn't have told your mom to say something like that now should you?" LOL. We laughed about that for the longest.

Back to Story

So, we're all snuggly and happy in our new home when the kids were at school one day and in between my bus route I receive a phone call, "Ma'am, we're sorry to tell you but you did not get approved for your house, you have to move out within ten days." I said, "Sir, please, you don't understand. My children are very happy here and we need a home. Please don't kick us out."

So I hung up the phone and went in the living room crying out to the Lord, "God please don't take this home from us. We love it here. We picked it out and decorated it Lord. Please! My children need a home!"

Then I went into intercession and worship. As I went back to my bedroom I receive a phone call that said UNIDENTIFIED. I thought, "Why doesn't it say unknown caller?" So I picked up the phone and this woman was singing *His Eye is on the Sparrow*. Well God knows that song is special between me and him because I've sang that over the years and it has ministered to many people.

I noticed that she sounded perfect. At first I thought it was Aunt Opal in Florida and I kept saying, "Aunt Opal? Aunt Opal?" After no answer I realized that this is God having an angel sing to me. So I sat and listened. I cried. The voice was so angelic and beautiful. Perfect soprano. I cried so hard!

Right after that call I receive another call, "Ma'am, I don't know what happened, but not only were you approved for the loan, but now your house note is cheaper and a better interest rate. Congratulations you do not have to move!" I shouted telling that man THANK YOU THANK YOU!

I ran in the living room to praise God! He allowed us to live in that home for one full year. y sons were preaching and winning their school for Christ. Northwest High School in Clarksville, TN. I also coached Freshman Cheerleading there as well.

In that home I sent my oldest son off to Bible College. I was so proud! My daughter wanted to go live with her dad soon after because she got tired of living with a preacher home so I let her go. He was single and they needed each other. So it ended up just me and Andrew in that home.

The Cost of Not Feeling Worthy

I started back to my old church. This is the same pastor that I took the youth to see 12 years earlier. He was an outreach man on fire for God and we had so many things in common then but I was married and we were only preaching partners from other towns. We hardly knew each other then. Over the years I would visit his church off and on and I finally ended up back at his church.

After a couple of years we developed a great friendship. He is single, nine years older than me, a virgin, and everyone knew he was married to the Lord and like celibate. However, we became best friends. I was so honest with him and I believe he's the first pastor that brought healing to my heart after all the other pastors has hurt me.

I would have sex with someone and go to the altar and confess. He would hold me close to him and say, "It's OK, we bind that soul-tie in Jesus name!" I remember him rubbing my hair at the altar and it always made my world seem better. He never held my sins against me. He would make me laugh like no other. Oh my God was he funny!

I was driving a school bus, had a son that was a senior in high school who was also conducting a Tuesday night prayer meeting with the youth of the city, and another son who was a sophomore who stood by him. They were a duo. Then I was coaching my daughter in cheerleading so we were always tight.

So, as our relationship developed into daily phone calls of prayer, laughter and just genuine friendship, I was the president of the bus drivers' union as well. He helped me greatly during that time period in my life.

So, we're best friends at the time when my son goes off to Bible College. Now I have less child support with two children gone and one to raise on a bus driver's income. The pressure is on to take care of my son and this new home.

I meet this guy and we have sex so we get married that day. He's sitting in the car with me when the pastor calls. He says, "Hello Junie, whatcha doing?"

(He always called me Junie…it always made me laugh).

I said, "Hello pastor, I have something to tell you. I got married today." He said, "I'm sorry, something must be wrong with the telephone line, and what did you say?" I repeated myself over and over again.

Finally he got real quiet. I said, "Hello, are you there?" He said, "Why would you do that to me?" I said, "To you? Oh, I'm sorry pastor; I should have let you marry us. Please forgive me. It was a last-minute decision." He said grievingly, "No, why would you do that to me?" Then I started crying and telling him how sorry I was that I hurt him. I thought in my heart that he was so devastated I didn't let him marry us.

So, when we got off the phone the new husband said, "Is your pastor single?" I said, "Yes, but he's celibate and a virgin. It's not like that, we're just best friends." He said, "No, He's in love with you! Your pastor is in love with you." I said, "No, he's not…he's just mad because he didn't marry us." So, I told him I had to go to the church and see him because I can't stand it thinking he's that mad at me. So, I left. I called four times and pastor wouldn't answer the phone so on the fourth one I told him that I was going to sit at the church all night and wait on him because I'd rather him hit me than to not talk to me.

Well he called me right back and said he would be there in five minutes.

When he got there he looked like the devil had beaten him to a pulp. He looked so sad. I apologized for hurting him by not allowing him to marry us.

After we went to his office he said, "Did you marry this guy so you can have sex with him?" I said, "Yes, I'm tired of fighting this thing!"

He said, "Just get an annulment, I'll pay for it. It was a dumb mistake you made and I will teach you how to be single."

So, I got home and husband had left and there was a note on the table, "I CAN'T COMPETE WITH YOUR PASTOR. HE'S IN LOVE WITH YOU." So, I called pastor and told him and he shouted, "YES, NOW WE CAN GET THE ANNULMENT AND ACT LIKE THIS NEVER HAPPENED! DON'T TELL ANYONE, IT WILL BE OUR SECRET!"

Yes, until he thought about what I did. He got so angry! He called me to a meeting with this other woman and chewed me out about it then called my voicemail for five days straight chewing me out. I would laugh at him cause I thought, "This man has lost his mind." He said on one call, "You ain't nothing but a Juanita Bynum. You can't keep it out of the sheets!" But he said it so mad. I laughed so hard over that one!

So, when I went back to church, someone told everyone in that church what I did. I began wearing the scarlet letter. Everyone hated me then. I was the whore of the church. My sins had been exposed.

It didn't stop me from meeting other men. I would just keep dating. I dated all the time.

The pastor wouldn't look at me anymore. He could hardly preach for weeks. It wrecked him pretty good.

He Is Jealous For Me Again

A year later I'm in the church (God wouldn't let me leave. I tried) and I was telling the ladies how I'm going on this date and this woman says, "I think God wants you all to himself." That statement made me so mad! I had forgotten all about God saying that twelve years earlier!

So, I yelled at God all the way home under the moonlight, "You're still asking me this twelve years later and five marriages later? Why are you asking me to do this? You see how codependent I am on men!

You see how I am about sex! Why can't you get a virgin or someone that hasn't had the life I have? Why me God?"

So that Sunday the pastor preached a sermon, "When God calls you to do something, He's going to equip you to do it." Then the Lord spoke to me and said, "June, if you will trust me, I will show you what a real husband is." I replied, "You can't have sex with me."

He said, "You will see how I will take care of you. Just trust me. I will help you." So, I said, "OK Lord, if you can take all this away, I will give you a try because my way is not working."

So, I went to the pastor and told him about my confrontation with God twelve years earlier and how I've been in disobedience which is why I married all these other men and I asked him if I could get baptized next Sunday with the others on Easter.

He said, "Yes, and I bear witness with this." So I called my son in Bible College and told him how I was in disobedience to God and it's because I don't believe I can be this woman and would he pray that I can do this and get baptized next Sunday. I told him I was marrying my true husband on Sunday.

I knew what it meant to get baptized again. In my heart I was marrying the TRUE husband who would never leave me or hurt me. However, I knew I would have to give up everything to marry Him. I knew I would have to give up my childhood dreams of having a family. I knew I would have to die to myself on everything I ever thought life meant to me.

Even when I was a little girl in all the shame and abuse I would dream of a family that was different. I wanted a dad to love me.

I wanted a mom home with me and who took care of me. I wanted true love. I could not understand WHY God did not want me to have that.

Why did He want me celibate and just living for Him? I had this battle raging on the inside but I knew my life was a failure the way I was doing it and I was so broken inside and needed to know the truth about a husband. Lord knows all the husbands in my life failed me. They did not give me what I was longing in my heart and mind.

I couldn't get enough sex. I couldn't get enough attention, satisfaction, love. I wasn't having sex with these men for the act of it. I was having sex for the love and attention I thought it brought to me.

It was all a lie and a false sense of love. I had no idea that a God I could not see or touch could provide all the natural needs I had. How could He feel this desire for sex? Attention? Intimacy? Best friend? I just couldn't see it. However, I'm ready to give Him a chance.

Dr. June Dawn Knight

6
I FOUND MY TRUE HUSBAND
AND CALL TO BIBLE COLLEGE

God Shakes World Harvest Bible College

My son calls me on that Thursday before baptism and says, "Mom you're not going to believe what happened in Missions Class today! There are about 100 students in there and as soon as class started the Holy Ghost came in the room and we all fell on our faces in intercession. Our professor walks in and says, 'There's a spirit of intercession in here for someone's family, who is it? It's you Brock, what's going on with your family?'" So Brock tells me that he told his class about my life and how I was marrying him that Sunday on Easter.

So the class got back on their faces and interceded for me for a whole hour. So my son told me that God told him to tell me that God is meeting me at church Sunday and that everything is going to be OK. I cried so hard!

My Wedding Day to the True Husband

On my way to church that morning I knew the baptism wasn't until that night, but I still rolled down the window and threw my cigarettes out! I said, "I'm done with you devil!"

So, when I got to church and during praise and worship, God just covered me like a glove. He wooed me and talked to me. He told me how much He loves me and how He's going to take care of me. I told Him, "Let's go!"

So after church I called all my family members and told them that I know I made a mockery of my life and why and asked them to come. They came.

I wore a white dress. This woman sang that song Alabaster Box. This song tore me up because it was like how I felt about my husband. I wanted to be a lover to him like I was all the other earthly men but more. I wanted to take my long hair and soak it in oil and wash his feet! I was gearing my passion away from men and sex to my first true love!

So, when I got baptized I testified to the church of my disobedience and asked them to forgive me. When I went under the water and come up I felt so clean. For the first time in my life I didn't feel the shame of the abuse, rape, and molestation. I felt clean! Wow!

The Call to Bible College - WHBC

Well after that, the Lord woke me up every morning at 4:00 a.m. to talk to me. Four days later the Lord woke me up and said, "Go to World Harvest Bible College." I said, "What God? I'm 36 years old! What do I do with this brand new house you gave me?" He said, "Sell your house and give away everything you have and follow me."

So I researched that Bible College and learned that they have a private prep school for my son to go to. It was expensive though, $4,500 for the tuition alone, much less all the other fees like uniforms, senior trips, etc. Then I was led by the Holy Spirit to study the kings of the Old Testament.

I did that for about five hours that day. Also, my daughter went to live with her dad because she got tired of living in a preacher home and she felt sorry for her dad because he was all alone. I let her go. So, I knew that for me to go to Bible College that I would have to leave her here and take only my son who is about to be a senior and he was class president and all. Also, he had been in that high school since his freshman year and I hated pulling him out on the best year of his life.

So, next morning the Lord wakes me up again, "I said Go to World Harvest Bible College!" I said, "OK Lord, if this is you, then I ask that you do like you did with Gideon. I was studying yesterday and you proved to him that it was you talking by him putting a fleece out there so I'm asking you that if you want me to ask my son to give up his senior year, sell my brand new home, and go to Bible College with nothing, then all I ask is that you pay my son's tuition through Harvest Preparatory School for $4,500. Once you pay that then I will know it's you that is calling me.

Well God worked it out for me to visit that church the next week. Rod Parsley was having a big Silent No More convention.

He wrote a book called *Silent No More* and this was the kick-off celebration.

When I got in the big banquet hall for the event with all the pastors from all over the world, I knew I was in a room full of greatness and I belonged. While I was sitting there this woman next to me that I didn't know touched

my shoulder and said, "God says that He has called you up here.

Don't worry about your son's tuition, God will take care of him." I looked at her like wow. Then next morning a woman walks up to me at the altar and says, "Thus sayeth the Lord, He has called you up here to go to Bible College. Don't worry about a thing, He will pay for it." Come to find out, that was the Missions Teacher that prayed for me a few weeks earlier!

So, I got the confirmation I needed. I went back and testified to the church and told them to come get my furniture. They did. Within two months I got an annulment, sold my house at cost, gave away everything I had and was packed up with nothing but boxes and a dime to my name in obedience to God. As we were leaving the house, we cleaned it spotless and were standing at the door holding hands to pray and we said, "God, we thank you for this beautiful home. You allowed us to live in this brand new home for a year. We knew it was never ours. It was yours. We pray you bless the next people that live here."

We got in the van and left!

7
MIRACLES AT WORLD HARVEST
BIBLE COLLEGE

Columbus Bound – Totally By Faith!

We are driving through Louisville and my mom calls, "June, how does it feel going to a city with nothing but a dime when you've never lived outside the State of Tennessee? How do you feel?" I said, "I feel great! I know God is waiting on me in Ohio!"

When we got there, we had an apartment waiting on us! People started giving us furniture!

First Blessing – Momma Parsley Anointing

My first service at the 12,000 seater church the Lord speaks to me and says, "Give Momma Parsley your diamond ring." I said, "This must be the devil! Why would God want me to give up my mother's inheritance ring? It's the only thing I have left of any value!" So, I didn't do it.

The next week God says it again. I ignore it.

Next week God says it again through Nassir Sidikki. He is preaching and he says, "Sometimes God will have you give up odd things to receive odd blessings." So after church I told my boys that I'm hearing God say the weirdest thing.

I told them what I'm hearing and they both said, "Momma, if God's telling you to do that then you must obey." They had such simple faith like, "Just do it mom!" LOL. God already asked me to give up my home, belongings, and all other material things to follow him to Bible College. I guess He wanted it all.

That night after battling with the Lord many weeks over giving up this inheritance ring, I decided to obey the Lord. All of a sudden here comes Momma Parsley! I have never seen her before or met her. You could just feel the power and authority she walked in! She walked on the platform from the right and interrupted the praise and worship and took the microphone.

She said, "I don't know who this is for, but the Lord spoke to me at 4:00 and told me to come to service tonight and tell SOMEONE that you must obey God and give me that diamond ring! I don't know why God has women give me their diamond rings! Look at my hands. Does it look like I need more rings? But, if that's you...you need to obey God!"

My children turned to me and went like BAM! In your face! LOL. Well, that was the confirmation I needed to obey God. I took the ring and put it in an offering envelope and wrote on the outside, "God, I'm believing you to pay Andrew's tuition to Harvest Prep for $4,500 and Brock's tuition to World Harvest Bible College for $1,100. I sealed that envelope. My pastor had paid my first year so I was taken care of.

So afterwards, they were having a prayer line and Brock said, "Come on mom, let's go get in line to get prayed for." Well, Momma Parsley was about six rows in front of us a few rows over and I replied to Brock, "Well, I think it's time to give Momma Parsley this diamond ring." Brock said, "Mom, you're not going to get to her through those security guards." I replied, "Well, I'm just gonna pray then."

So, he walked off and I bowed my head and said, "OK Lord, if you want me to give her this diamond ring, you're going to have to open the door cause it's not like I can just throw it at her." I looked up and a man was standing in front of me.

He said, "Momma wants to see you." MY HEART FELL TO THE FLOOR!

I walked over behind her where they told me to stand and she turned around and I about fainted! I mean I had never stood before greatness until that moment. The power that exuded from this woman was amazing!

She looked at me and said, "The Lord said you needed to see me."

I said, "Yes ma'am. I am 36 years old, from Clarksville, Tennessee and the Lord told me to sell my house and give away everything I had to come to Bible College. I have nothing left and He told me to give you the last thing I own."

She looked at the envelope that had written on it:

"God, I'm believing you to pay Andrew's tuition to Harvest Preparatory School in the amount of $4,500 and I'm believing for you to pay Brock's tuition through the Bible College for $1,100."

96

She looked at the ▪writing, ripped the envelope open and put that ring on the ONE FINGER THAT DIDN'T HAVE A RING! IT LOOKED LIKE IT MATCHED IT TO A T! I MEAN it matched the other rings and fit her finger perfectly! I was amazed! She touched my forehead and said, "Receive". Man I went flying back!

I didn't know what happened at the moment; but let me tell you what happened since that encounter!

The Miracle Summer –
God Paid Tuitions - Andrew's Miracle

Two weeks later God supernaturally paid my son Andrew's tuition through Harvest Prep! How did He do it? Well, he was working at Hobby Lobby and his boss was a Christian. One day his boss took him to lunch and said, "Andrew, you're practicing football at the most expensive private school in Columbus right?" Andrew replied, "Yes."

Boss says, "How can your mom afford that?" Andrew says, "She's believing God to pay it. We came up here with nothing but boxes, with nowhere to live and God supplied an apartment as soon as we arrived. We're

just believing God to pay it." (Then told him whole story).

So next day the boss takes him to lunch again and says, "Let's make a pit-stop". Drives him to Harvest Prep and takes him in the office and says, "How much does this boy owe you?" They said,

"$4,500 for tuition." The man says, "I want to pay all additional fees too...how much?" They said, "Well, there's senior fees, pictures, class trip, uniforms, field trips, etc." The man wrote out a check and paid it all! Yes, you heard it...FAR ABOVE WHAT I ASKED GOD FOR!

Then the man took him shopping and bought him a wardrobe of clothes AND A CAR! Yes he did! Then...he invited us to dinner. I asked him why he did that for my son and he said, "Well, when I interviewed your son, he kept saying 'yes sir' and that blessed me because I don't hear that much in the North. Then when I took him to lunch and heard your story, I'm a Christian and the Lord spoke to me and told me to take care of your son his senior year!" I greatly thanked him.

Then after dinner he asked us to follow him. He took us to a furniture store. The Lord knows that a kitchen table is my most prized piece of furniture because I believe the breakdown of the American family is when they got away from the dinner table. I am a cook and really treasured those family times. So, the man takes us in this furniture store and says, 'Pick out any kitchen table set you want!" I was like, WHAT? LOL.

I had it set in my heart to use rot iron and glass since my kids were grown. So, not only did he buy the table, but he bought the coffee table, end tables, lamps, etc. to match it!

So that's how God answered the request about Andrew.

Brock's Miracle!

Well Brock had already been in Bible College for a year and was a leader in the youth group at World Harvest Church. So a couple weeks later he goes to youth camp as a leader and had nine boys under him so it was a team of 10. They were competing all week in a Survivor Camp for $1,000 which meant each player would receive $100 if they won.

Well our family is beasts at competitions (LOL). We all were sports players so Brock was natural for this. Well his team won...so when he came back to church that next service a woman found us and she said:

Hello, I'm so and so from Cincinnati (about two hours south) and my son was in your group. My husband and I are both Plastic Surgeons. When we sent our son to camp he was a heathen. He had been in and out of jail, in constant trouble, doing drugs, etc. So, we sent him as a last-ditch effort. When he comes home he was a different boy and now he's preaching the gospel, on-fire for God and no bitterness in his heart. He's a totally different boy! So, we want to bless you Brock and pay your tuition!

SHE PAID IT! Then she sent the boys on a shopping spree at Lifeway Christian Book Store, and then paid for my son's honeymoon!

First Day of School

Well, the summer ended and we all had great jobs. We made good money and was totally enjoying ourselves in this new culture. One of the first shocks when we arrived in Columbus was seeing openly gay people.

We had never seen that before and our first Sunday we were at a gas station and these two men were walking in the gas station holding hands. We sat in the car with our mouths to the floor. We were like, "What is that?" LOL. We couldn't believe it. We didn't see that in the South.

Anyways, the first day of school God shut us all down. Brock's car blew up meaning engine went out. Andrew's car tore up and mine did too.

It was the strangest thing! My car would only drive us one mile down the road to Bible College/church and back. If we tried to go other places it would shut down. God made it very apparent!

So, this began the pit process. We all lost our jobs so we were just totally living off of child support. Well our apartment was $750 a month and child support was only like $800 a month. So, we were lacking already. Soon after, ex-husband moves a woman in and quits paying child support too! So, God cut us off from all support and made me rely on Him 100%.

The Momma Anointing

So, needless to say, God overwhelmingly blessed my requests! But even more than that is what He did for me spiritually! When Momma Parsley imparted into me, she gave me that motherly anointing! I didn't know it at the time, but it became very apparent soon after.

 When my first classes started, I was one of the oldest students. The other 500 (about) students clung to me. It partly had to do with the favor they had for Brock...but most of it was the impartation from Momma P. I had 500 students calling me Momma June all the time. Here are some facts about that experience:

They came to me with their problems and I would pray and encourage them back to victory! I received so much loving from the students that I never thought about sex again. It fulfilled all I was looking for. This in combination with the peace I had with God. Since I came back from Bible College, God has asked me to impart into other ministers this motherly anointing.

The Cheer Call

I'm riding down the road from school one day and pastor's wife called me and said, "Pastor and I was talking and we heard that you are a championship cheerleading coach." I said, "Yes ma'am." She said, "We would like for you to consider coaching for Harvest Prep."

So, that afternoon I was walking down the hall at World Harvest Church (Harvest Prep was upstairs) and Rod Parsley was sitting down on the left with some of his staff. He yelled at me, "June Knight, come here." I said, "Yes sir." So, I stood before him and he didn't say anything. He just stared at me for like two minutes. I knew in the spirit that he was examining my spirit. He was reading my mail. So I stood there nervously and he said, "You're hired." Then I said, "thank you sir." Then I walked off.

Well come to find out their daughter was on the team so that's why they were so picky about who they chose. I also began driving a school bus for them and also had the honor to drive the Bible College students on trips. We had so much fun on those trips!

No Money and No Provision

God knows to the extent of what my old man (previous to the call) would do to survive. If I got too desperate I would have sugar daddies to help me. You ask how that started? Well let me tell you how Satan moved in.

First of all, after being molested as a young girl, then only having men take advantage of my beauty and body over the years, I quickly learned how to turn that around for my advantage.

So, God knew what I would do to survive. So, now that God was my husband and He wanted to show me that He is my supplier and will meet all my needs including sexual, then He put me to the test!

Well, He made me go three months with no money. Yes, we were on food stamps, but that's it. We ended up being three months behind on rent.

By the time December rolled around, everything was collapsing! They were shutting our water off, lights, phones and we had received three eviction notices. Also, I had one payment left on my van. I had paid on that thing for five years and God would not release that last $500 payment to pay it off! Everything was swirling around me!

Unworthiness Rearing Its Ugly Head Again

The Bible College required we wore suits so after I wore all my hand-me-downs, I had one ugly dress left. It was SO UGLY. It was green and orange. For a big woman, this is not attractive. I thought, "I will wear this dress because I sing in the choir and no one will see me."

I arrived on that Sunday morning about 8:30 a.m. and the choir director said, "We are not sitting up here today, we are singing on the platform AND with no choir robes on." My heart sank. However I thought, I will just hide in between and no one will see this ugly dress. Then the choir director informs us that we are not coming back up to the choir loft, but we are sitting with the congregation.

After ministering through praise and worship, we sat in front of Pastor Parsley to the right of the platform (if you're standing looking out to the congregation). I made sure I sat in the middle of the huge choir so no one would see me again.

In the middle of PRP's (Pastor Rod Parsley = PRP) sermon, he said, "Church, we need church busses. I need you to give so we can get new busses." Being that I was a bus driver for him and knew he was telling the truth, I yelled out, "Amen Pastor!" He heard me.

He stopped his sermon and said, "You! Stand up." I looked around like, "Lord please don't let that be me." He said again, "June Knight, stand up." I stood up in so much shame over what I was wearing. He instructed the congregation, "I want everyone to sit down around her and I WANT ALL CAMERAS ON HER!" I wanted to faint. Not today. Please. Of all days! I looked up and saw myself on the big screens and wanted to run and hide. I saw my ugly dress on all the big screens and all you see is a sea of orange green and yellow. Can I say ugly! I was horrified!

After everyone sat down, he said something like this (It's been 7 or 8 years)…"This woman volunteers more than anyone in this church.

She just arrived her a few months ago and already involved in everything.

She drives our school bus, coaches our cheerleaders at Harvest Preparatory School, was a Competition Champion Cheer Coach, goes to World Harvest Bible College, etc."

So, while he's proclaiming, Momma Parsley walks up to the platform and says, "Call her up here to tell her testimony! God done an amazing thing to get her up here!" I looked at PRP with so much shame and shook my head like...NO PLEASE...NO. He looked at me and thought about it for a minute, then said, "Maybe some other time." He had mercy on me.

After the service I had hundreds of people coming up to meet me and I could literally just sink in the ground wanting to hide because of this dress! Needless to say, I threw that dress away and never wore it again!

The Prodigal Daughter Came Home!

It was so hard living in another state without my daughter. I had coached

her in cheerleading for about 10 years by this point and she had made the high school cheerleading squad at her dad's town. It was the first time she was under another coach and here I was in Ohio coaching another high school squad. It just didn't seem right coaching without her there.

See, Meagan always thought she was the odd one because her brothers were superpowers. LOL. They were well-known preachers in Clarksville and she felt like she didn't have any gifts. I knew that I dedicated her to the Lord as soon as she entered the world and knew she was special, but didn't know her calling.

Her brothers always protected her like a hawk. She was beautiful and men would gawk at her all the time so the boys would keep their eyes out for her. This is one reason she wanted to live with her dad is because she got tired of living in a preacher home. She also felt sorry for her dad because he was single and lonely. This is what she told me anyway.

Her dad had become a good dad after we divorced. He calmed down and began spending more time with the kids, etc.

I never tried to keep them from him or put him down to them. I respected his position as their father.

Anyways, she went to live with him and as far as I knew everything was fine. Until I prayed for her one day and the Holy Spirit revealed something about my daughter. I couldn't believe it. It hurt so bad I thought it was the devil telling me something like that.

So, the next day I received a phone call from her cousin confirming what the Holy Spirit told me! I am so thankful the Holy Spirit always warns me before bad news comes. Anyways, I found out that her dad moved this woman in the house a few months earlier. I knew that things probably were not working out with that woman living there.

I called my daughter and said, "Is there something you need to tell me young lady?" She said nervously, "NO." I said, "You know the Holy Spirit tells me everything, I'm just waiting to hear it from you." She confessed. So I demanded to talk to her father.

It ended up that I insisted that he send her up to Ohio and give her back to me. He said no at first but finally agreed. I was so happy!

We are the Bride is Born

My son, Brock, started a youth ministry back in the early 2000's called Wildfire. He had the vision of uniting the youth groups across the city. It was very successful. Well, one night I was in worship at one of his meetings and the Lord gave me a vision:

It was in a big coliseum/arena and it was very dark. All of a sudden the black lights shined on the stage and there was a bride standing there. All you could see was her white painted lips, around her eyes was painted like a butterfly, her nails were white, and her hair was long and glitter all in her hair. You couldn't tell WHO it was; just a bride. Under the black lights her whiteness glowed (nails, eyes, lips, etc.). A video started playing on the screen to the left of her life and abuse. Then worship music started playing and she worshiped the Lord so beautifully! It was like she was desperately waiting for her groom to come get her. Then all of a sudden he appeared in a tux! They did a dance together...then they both disappeared.

So, now I'm in Bible College and I was on the platform with the Bible College Choir.

As I entered deep worship (I call it entering the throne room)....I had an encounter with the Lord....

The Lord said, "Do you remember that vision of the bride?" I replied, "Yes Lord." He said, "That is YOU." I said, "What? She was skinny!" He said, "Yes, you will write a book called 'We Are The Bride' and tell the world what I am showing you about being the Bride of Christ and I'm the True Husband." I wept in unbelief. Here I am...the woman that had been married

six times! Why would I write a book about being the Bride of Christ? I replied, "Lord, I don't even have a high school education much less write a book!" So, I come out of the throne room.

Then as we come off platform...we sat down to hear the speaker...then next thing you know, Rod Parsley comes storming in the chapel. He said, "I don't know who this is for...but the Lord interrupted my plans today and told me to COME PREACH TO YOU THAT WE ARE THE BRIDE!!!!! Yes!!! He preached the whole time about it! I cried so hard!!! We are the Bride Ministries was born that day in my heart. God planted the seed and Rod Parsley came behind Him and watered that seed.

God's Miracle to Meagan

At this end of this chapel I walked up to Rod Parsley and said, Thank you pastor for that word! He grabbed my hand and said, "June, I heard your daughter is moving up here. Why is she not living with you? I was so embarrassed! I told him how she didn't want to be living in a preacher home so she wanted to live with her sinner father. I asked him to pray with me that God would pay her tuition too so that she can go to school with us.

He said, "I'll pay for it and I'll buy her uniforms!" I told him that she was a championship cheerleader and asked him if she could be on the squad too and that I have coached her all her life. He said yes! I told him we had one extra uniform! It was just perfect!

So, my son Brock went to get her in Louisville, KY and it was on a Friday night. It was a dream come true. The cheerleaders were so excited about her coming and wanted her on the team. So I'll never forget looking at the prodigal daughter and seeing the shame on her face. I just grabbed her and  gave her the biggest hug! Oh, to hold my baby again! All the cheerleaders said hello and told her they was excited she was going to be cheering with them.

The Bible College students all knew about her because of me and Brock. So, she got plenty of loving from them too and welcoming her home. I grabbed her hand and took her up the bleachers to meet PRP. When we got to the top I said, "Meagan, meet Pastor Rod Parsley."

He threw his arms open and said, "Come here Meagan, welcome home! This is your home! We love you." So he loved on her and gave her a bear hug. Ms. Joni hugged her too and welcomed her. So, she was shocked to see all the loving and acceptance she received. It was her promise land too. She instantly made all kinds of friends and had a busy social life. She got on the cheer squad and the uniform fit her perfectly. She would walk in the church for services and ten girls would run up to her, "Meagan!" She loved it there.

God Touched Meagan!

Meagan loved the youth services and one night when I went to pick her up the youth came running up to me. This was in November.

By this time she had seen and experienced a different mother. No longer did I have boyfriends. No longer was I dependent on men.

No longer was I living for myself. I was all about God and my family.

So, the kids came running up to me and said, "Momma June, you need to come to the altar now." It kind of scared me. They said, "You'll see. Meagan needs you." So, I got there and she turned around and it was the most beautiful sight I had ever seen! My daughter had repentance all over her face. It was covered in snot and tears. She said, "I'm so sorry mom for everything I've done to you! I'm so sorry!" Then she laid her head on my shoulders and cried like a baby. It was a very intimate moment between me and her. I knew she was in the presence of the Lord. We forgave each other.

Testifying to a 7th Grade Class

This teacher at Harvest Prep invited me to come in and teach her class one day. She asked me to share my story to inspire her students.

So, I did and they were all crying. I told them how I had been married six times searching for the love that only God can bring. I told them how jealous God was over me and that He wanted me all to myself.

It was an honor to share with them. They asked all kinds of questions about my children, etc.

Confrontation with the Parsleys

Being that I had coached in public schools and was used to their policies I just coached this team the way I knew how. Well there was this girl on the team that purposely didn't show up to Saturday's practice for the Pep Rally. We learned our dance in one practice; she was not there so I benched her for Pep Rally.

So, we're setting up for pep rally and we're about 10 minutes from starting and here comes PRP (Pastor Rod Parsley), and Ms. Joni. Man did she look mad! She walked up to me and chewed me out in front of everyone! She was all in my face saying, "You don't bench people in a private school! They pay for their education! Etc."

So, I took the rebuke and tried softly to explain about us doing a dance and learning it in one practice, etc. She wouldn't listen. She was so mad. I knew she was stressed because PRP's sister was very sick in California and they flew out there to see her and just got back.

PRP was standing behind her and I could tell how mad he was at me too. I was so embarrassed but I took it. They went to sit down and we started.

Well when we did the dance, the school had never seen anything like this so they absolutely loved it! We got a standing ovation! I could tell the Parsley's loved it too!

Afterwards they came back to me and repented. Ms. Joni told me how tired she was and how she got bombarded when she got off the plane and she was sorry she took it out on me. She also told me how much she loved that dance routine, etc.

Because of how I took the rebuke in public, I got promoted. I don't remember how exactly but I remember them telling me how much they respected me that I took that like a champ and didn't get offended.

Favor with the Parsleys

My family had so much favor with PRP and Ms. Joni. Meagan spent the night with their daughter many times and PRP would fix them breakfast. One morning Meagan said that she was sneaking down the stairs for a drink and fell down the steps. PRP was standing there and asked her if she was OK. LOL. She got busted. It was so funny she said. He then proceeded to cook her breakfast and talk to her.

Then, their daughter and my son Andrew went to Homecoming together. PRP rented them a limo and they rode with a bunch of friends. They had the time of their lives. We still laugh about it to this day because the boys

protected their sister. Whenever a guy would try to dance with her they would walk in between them and say, 6 inches dude, and 6 inches! Man we laughed about that for years!

I drove the HP students over to their house and they would go swimming and have parties there. Their home is beautiful and in the country. Nothing too fancy.

My Confrontation with God

Now we're back to the eviction notices and everything crashing around me. Well one night on a Saturday night I had all I could take. I couldn't sleep so I drove to the church at 1:00 a.m. in my pajamas to have a pow-wow with God. I sat in my van in the parking lot looking at all the nation's flags.

The church would put them out every Saturday for Sunday services. At that time I didn't know how prophetic this confrontation was.

Anyways, I told God, "God, you called me up here and asked me to give up my life to follow you. I did that. I gave up everything for you. I haven't had sex in almost a year and this is the longest I've ever gone without sex! You helped me to overcome! Now I know a husband wouldn't do me like this.

You said that you would show me what a real husband is! I know a husband provides a home for his Bride! I know a husband makes sure the family has food on the table. GOD WHERE ARE YOU AT? I'm at the end of my rope! I have three kids depending on me God! Please help me! I don't know why you're doing all this but I'm just going to praise you anyways!" So I drove back home.

Calamity Comes!

That morning we're driving to church and the car runs out of gas halfway there! Here we are all dressed in our suits walking down the highway! Traffic stops both ways because they all knew us! Here are all the things we were involved with at World Harvest Church:

Harvest Prep Cheer Coach & Bus Driver

WHBC Bus Driver

Metro Harvest Outreach Team

WHC Choir

IN WHBC with oldest son

Son is Senior at HP and daughter is freshman there!

So needless to say, we were very involved in the church's culture. So, people said, "Knight Family, what are ya'll doing walking down the road?" I started yelling in frustration, "You tell me! We've got three eviction notices, everything's falling apart, etc.!

So they said, "Give us the key to your van and they took us to church. They ended up filling the van up with gas which cost them about $80. I was like, "Wow...God really blessed us with a full tank of gas!" Until I got home and got a phone call.

"Ma'am, we are coming in one hour to repossess your van for non-payment. Can you meet us at the store?" So, they took my car. Now that was like my last straw! We had to hitch a ride to church. At church I just threw my hands up and praised the Lord!

God Opened The Heavens!

The next day this man walked up to me at Bible College and said, "Knight Family, I don't know what's going on with ya'll, but the Lord woke me up this morning at 4:00 a.m. and told me to pay all of your bills. Now, what's going on?" So, I told him the story. He paid almost $10,000 in one day!

This is what he blessed us with:

Paid past three months' rent and up three months at $750 each

Paid $600 to fix my son's car so we could have a vehicle

Bought the boys a bunkbed for like $800. It was a nice wood one.

Bought us lots of clothes and coats.

Paid all of our bills off

Then he called me next day and said that him and his wife were talking and wanted to know who I was taking to the Winter Formal on Friday night. Did I have a date? Their winter formal is like a prom.

Well normally I would have a date but I told him, "I think my date will be my three children." So, he said that they wanted to bless me and my daughter for the formal. They wanted to get our hair and nails done and buy us pretty outfits.

Every day that week people gave us money. Favor just poured out everywhere! That Friday morning the Lord woke me up at 4:00 a.m. and said, "Because you gave up your house and car for me, I am going to bless you with a better house and car that you could ever dream of!" I said, "Wow God! Thank you. It will have to be a nice house because I've had nice houses!"

When I arrived at WHBC that morning a student walked up and handed me $20. So, I called the kids and told them that I wanted us to go eat lunch.

When I went to pick up Andrew and Meagan, the teacher that I spoke in her class walked up and handed me a beautiful mirror box.

She said, "You inspired my children so much that they made this for you. Thank you for speaking in my class." I was so blessed!

So when we went to the restaurant we were all sitting there reading the cards from the children. They were saying things like, "Thank you for telling me your story.

My mom was like you and I told her your story and now she has quit having boyfriends and is trusting God."

"Thank you for telling me your story; I cry every night because I miss my mother who left me for another man. Now I pray for her." We all just cried reading these letters.

While we're reading them four Bible College students walk in and start yelling, "Momma June! We love you!" Then one of them handed me a piece of paper. I opened it and it was a check for $1,000.

I slid it across the table to my daughter and when she opened it and saw it she started crying and said, "Why is God doing all this for us? I'm overwhelmed with all the blessings!" This reply is how this book is born.

I said, "Because I obeyed God and this is where your wealth is. Obeying God is where your wealth is!"

So we left the restaurant and had a girl's day out. We got all fixed up for the prom that night.

God Made Me Queen

When we arrived at the Bible College, they had it all decked out like winter wonderland. I walked in with one son on each arm and Meagan on the end. We walked in on the red carpet with white trees lining the sides all the way to the end. We felt like royalty walking in. I can't explain that moment of walking in with my kids versus some man. They were the best date a mother could ever hope for!

Well the Bible College kids were on the end of the red carpet flashing their cameras taking pictures of us like we was in Hollywood saying, "Wow Knight Family! Ya'll look so beautiful! Look at you Momma June! Wow! Etc." It was a moment I will never forget. I was so proud to be shining with my kids.

Then we danced the night away. We had so much fun! I always got so much loving and the kids all treated me like one of them so I could party with the best of them! LOL. God just really prepared me for that night like Esther before the King!

Well it came time to vote for King and Queen. I thought Brock should be King so I voted for him and this other girl. When it came time to announce it they said, for King it's Matthew! I always loved him. They said it was a close call between him and Brock but Matthew won! I was still happy!

But then, they voted me as Bible College Queen at the Winter Formal my 1st Semester! I couldn't believe it!

When I walked up on the platform to sit on the chair and get crowned, I

turned around and looked at my proud children and that look will never leave my heart. To see them admiring their new mother. A woman totally trusting in God and now He's rewarding her for the faithfulness. I felt so special to be in front of the 500 people who actually loved me. Wow.

So, we left that night and went to a restaurant with 12 other students and I was telling them how God woke me up that morning to tell me that about giving me a new home and car. About 30 minutes later this man walked in and Brock said, "Hey! Didn't you used to go to the Bible College? I want you to meet my mother; God just brought her up here from Tennessee." The man stops in his tracks and across from the restaurant he points and me and declares, "Thus sayeth the Lord, because you gave up your house and car for me, I will bless you with a better house and car than you could ever dream of." All the 12 at the table's mouths dropped to the floor. They were in awe how God just confirmed it in front of them!

So, I told them it will be a mansion! LOL. Me and the kids went home that night and dreamed about this new home!

My Christmas Present from God

A few weeks later God wakes me up on Christmas Eve at 4:00 a.m. and says, "I have a present for you." I laughed and said, "Oh yeah, what?" He said, "I'm going to let you get married again." I was in shock and angry at same time. I said, "Why would you do that now after all I've been through! I don't even want a husband now because you do everything for me and I don't need one! I don't have to do anything and you take care of my bills, etc." God said, "You had to love me before you could ever love a man."

Oh my God! I realized I had my priorities in the wrong order.

I then greatly repented and told God how sorry I was that I put men before him! He said, "You will meet your husband before Christmas of next year."

So, I go to church and God confirms it twice. This woman in the choir

said, "Thus sayeth the Lord…" Then I go out to the congregation and this random person walks up and says, "Thus sayeth the Lord…"

The Miracle of Meagan and Tommy Bates

I was so excited to start the New Year off in 2006! God has promised me a home, car, and husband. Not that material things are the point, but that I had a new life coming. I was so excited! Our family was perfect…we were all so happy in Ohio! Meagan just got saved and was totally on fire for God. Brock was very active at Bible College and did outreach all the time. Andrew was a senior at Harvest Prep and was having the time of his life! I was the Queen of the Bible College…the momma…God had all my bills paid, and I loved my job at the church. I loved my life too.

When Tommy Bates held a revival at WHC in January, it was so amazing! One night he said, "There is a boy in the back of the sanctuary in that section and if you don't give your heart to God tonight, you will die. Tonight is your last night to live!"

I've never heard anyone say that prophetically so I feared for that boy. He was telling him that he better get his life right with God! All the kids from that area came up front but one! He refused to. Well, he died that night. He stole his mom's car and partied all night then had a head-on collision and died.

One of the elders, Elder Bronson, was riding by and saw them loading his dead body in the ambulance and remembered seeing him at the service the night before and remembered that word. He pulled over and begged them to let him pray for the boy. They told him it was too late that he had died. However, they let him in the ambulance. He prayed and cried out to God to have mercy on this boy. Nothing happened so he got in his car and left. They took the boy to the hospital then about an hour later. HE COMES BACK TO LIFE! He was already in the morgue!

So, he comes to the revival that night testifying about how he asked God to have mercy on him and give him another chance. Man the church was rejoicing!

Then that night about 2,000 young people came to the altar and got filled with the Holy Spirit. My daughter was one of them. It was an amazing night! The next day at school she couldn't stop praying in tongues. She and two other girls were still praying in tongues so that teacher sent them to the bathroom. They started praying for girls and they started getting slain in the spirit all over the bathroom.

Then the teachers knew something was going on so they moved them to the conference room which held about 100 people. God just interrupted classes and students were coming in there for them girls to pray for them. So, it ends up that the whole floor is full of students who were laid out crying, speaking in tongues and having a genuine experience with God.

Then they called PRP. They told him that these three girls were interrupting classes to pray. So Pastor Parsley told them to shut down the whole school. He wanted them three girls to pray for every teacher, student, and every person at Harvest Prep. My daughter said she prayed for six hours! She said she has never prayed so much! It was a miracle!

They were all in the big sanctuary and little 3rd graders were running around the church shouting. Teachers were speaking in tongues for the first time, etc. It was just a big blow-out in the Holy Spirit! Then they brought pastor's son in there who has autism.

He doesn't let anyone touch him. However, Meagan said when they touched him to pray for him, he spoke in tongues for the first time! It was a miracle!

When she called to tell me all this…I couldn't wait to get to church that night!   I couldn't wait to hear what PRP was going to say! He was always transparent about the struggles with his son, so I knew we would all be rejoicing with him!!

I tell you what…it was the most amazing night! Here comes Rod Parsley to the right of the platform and he rolled all the way across the platform screaming! "My dream come true! My son was filled with the Holy Ghost today! My school experienced revival!" Man…he was so happy. He told the church what happened and the whole church broke out in the craziest revival!

After that, they started calling Meagan "Prophetess Meagan." She was so happy until the devil moved in about five months later!

The Enemy Came in Like a Flood

Since I did not want my daughter growing up doing the things I've done in the past with men, I was trying to do a bible study with her about being single. At this time the devil comes in like a flood.

She hardly ever heard from her dad after she moved to Ohio. But one day he called her and said, "I'm marrying that woman and I don't want anything else to do with you. Don't call me again."

I mean he just said this out of the blue. I don't know if the future wife told him to choose between daughter and her or what. However, I do know how it tore my daughter up.

The devil came after my daughter's calling. She did not handle this rejection well at all. She went through a lot after that for about six months. It about sucked the life out of her.

International Nights at My Apartment

During the time that I'm battling my daughter's issues and trying to keep peace in the house, I'm hosting the Bible College kids at my apartment every Saturday night for dinners. It ended up being about 75 kids every weekend so we started doing theme nights like Latino night, Island night, etc.

However, the best night was Southern night. LOL. That's where I fried everything! Tomatoes, potatoes, chicken, cornbread, etc.

The kids loved it because it made them feel like they were coming home to momma's every weekend. They would be in the parking lot throwing the football, playing around, etc. We had so much fun!

We learned so much about culture. Once we knew that next week would be a certain night like Italian night, on Sunday morning I would get the ingredient list from the Italians who were cooking the next Saturday night. So, I would take the list to Bible College and tell the students, "We need tomatoes, bread, etc." They would each volunteer to bring something and they would bring it to my apartment by Friday night.

Then on Saturday morning the Italians would come and cook all day. We had worship music playing and we had the best time!

So, when the other students arrived that night, they would eat this culture's food then they would talk to all of us about their culture and preach. IT WAS AWESOME!!!

When I knew things were spiraling out of control with my daughter I asked the students to please pray for me because I didn't want to leave Bible College. My daughter got so sick. She lost so much weight. She went from a size 7 to a size 0. I couldn't stand watching her suffer.

Had to Leave my Queen Hood

I say it was my Queen Hood because I was so happy there. God paid all my bills and I had it made! I had so much loving from the other students and favor all the way around!

Anyways, after much suffering on my daughter's part, the stress of it all, me not trusting God to finish it out, I left and came back to Tennessee.

I was only two months away from meeting my husband, getting my new house, etc.

However, I couldn't stand watching her suffer and I wanted to get her away from the situation and stress. He was the devil himself; or rather the devil was using him against my daughter.

So, I was so devastated that when I crossed the state line that I bought a pack of cigarettes. I hated to go back to Egypt! I felt like my life was over. I wasn't so much mad at my daughter as I felt so out of control with everything.

Back to Egypt

When we came back to Nashville, we tried living with my mother. However, that was short-lived. The only person that would take me in was my old partying buddy. Me and Meagan moved in with her and I slowly began to compromise my beliefs and I went back to the bars. In the meantime I go back to my old church a failure again.

So, needless to say pastor wouldn't look at me anymore, much less they wouldn't allow me to talk to him anymore and it was this way for seven more years. For seven years I'm miserable. In and out of church, partying, etc. Then I go back to college determined I'm going to finish it!

Now in Secular College

I went back to get my Bachelor's Degree and started out wanting to be a high school history teacher, but after I saw how they wanted them to be extremely liberal and they basically pushed me out because I was conservative, I changed my major to public relations. I thought that it would help me even in the ministry if God called me back out.

I started noticing that 42% of the college students were older people but

they didn't have anything for us, so I talked some other students into making it a class project to start a non-traditional honor society.

So I became the president and they still have it today! Then I started a non-traditional student society to where we could change the culture.

I produced a documentary to expose how the older students felt there. Well, the college ended up offering me a graduate assistant position and paid for me to go to Graduate School.

I graduated with my Bachelors at 3.54. I was on the Dean's List 7 out of 9 semesters!

Then while I was in graduate school studying Corporate Communications I went to London and the school paid for most of it! I studied under the top three global advertising and marketing firms in the world. I was there three weeks during winter of 2011/2012.

So, I was able to be there New Year's Eve 2012! It was London Olympic Year and Queen's Jubilee. It was very historical!

While I was in London I discovered that they are already chipping people with the human implantation chip!

I asked my professors from the University of Kentucky if I could write my paper using that product.

We had to write a paper comparing a product and how they market in Europe versus the United States. After I wrote this 20-page paper, I ended up making a 100 and even made a 100 in my class!

My boss was so impressed that he offered to send me to get my doctorate in Corporate Communications at the University of Illinois and he was going to pay for it! He said that no student of his in 30 years has ever made a 100 on a study abroad class and told me how smart I was.

So I told him I had to pray about it because that's a big decision.

I was already teaching some classes and helping him teach and grade papers. I truly enjoyed my college years. At this time I was working for a lawyer full-time, working at the college (Austin Peay State University), president of three organizations, finishing my paper, and a full-time student. So, I love

having a lot on my plate...especially when I enjoy it.

Also, while working for that lawyer I bought myself a brand new Toyota Camry because I was so sure of my future and success.

So, after praying about it, I heard God plainly said, "NO!" So, I went back to my boss and told him God's answer and he got so mad! He said, "I don't understand why God would have you give up your future like that? Give up 100,000 education? Etc." So, my last semester he sat me down every day in the office and tried to convince me that my religion was crazy and that I should reconsider my decision.

One day I just told him firmly, "Sir, my family is different, we're all called of the Lord and God has a plan for us." So it ends up that I graduated early because I took too many classes and didn't know it. I graduated after a year and a half in grad school.

I graduated with honors because I only made one B and that was in my first research class because it was so hard! However, when I went to pick up my degree in the spring they had stripped me of my honors! They deducted one point! I tried to fight it but they said no! I couldn't believe it!

*Austin Peay State University Master's Degree
Graduation December 2012*

Graduation with Bachelor's Degree in Public Relations August 2011

LOU ENGLE & THE CALL 07/07/07

Lou Engle from The Call Ministries called us one day. He heard about what happened with my daughter at Harvest Preparatory School. He invited her to be one of the guest speakers on the platform at the 07/07/07 event. She was so nervous. In her heart she knew she wasn't right with God and what this meant to minister in front of thousands of people. However, she still stepped up to the plate.

I was so proud of her and couldn't wait to hear her speak. She never spoke. She came back to our seats at the end of the day and said they ran out of time didn't have enough time for her to speak. However, I knew it was God's mercy on her because she wasn't ready. So, I was still honored that Lou Engle even knew her name and her story!

8
THE PIT STARTED

Following graduation in December of 2012, I went on a Bahama Cruise as a gift to myself. Following the vacation, I applied for over 450 jobs. So from January to April I started out working a temporary job at APSU, then I worked for my ex-brother-in-law a couple of months, but God just wouldn't open the door. Then one day I heard God say, "Get back in the prayer closet and get right with me!"

So on May 8, 2013 I got back in the prayer closet and laid my sadness down at the cross. I finally faced God and quit running from Him. I finally told Him how sad I was at the way everything happened. I also drew a line in the sand and told the devil I was done with him! He wasn't taking me or my children for another ride! So, I began the spiritual warfare...

My Saul Conversion/ My Death to the Old Man/ My Will

I have been single for 12 years now and been married 6 times (one annulled), and went to Bible College after all the failures. God showed me how he wants to be my TRUE husband. While in Bible College, I quit and came back to Nashville because I could not stand to watch my daughter suffer. When it was me suffering I could handle it. Since then it's been seven years.

My heart has been so devastated about my failure at Bible College I haven't been able to pick myself back up. I found the strength May 8, 2013. I went back to my prayer closet where I left my spiritual husband years ago. I told him "I surrender. You can have it all! My master's degree, my new car, my new apartment, all my material things, my children, my dreams, my hopes...MY EVERYTHING. I'M DONE. Please accept me back."

Since that time, my life has been crazy! He had shut every door in my life since I graduated and he KEPT THOSE DOORS SHUT! He wanted me to spend time with Him. During this time I spent night and day seeking his face! I cut off ALL CABLE...no news, no worldly music; I mean everything attached to this world. I spent one to eight hours a day in prayer.

Even when I wasn't praying, I was listening to preaching, worship, and

meditating. I pursued him with all of my heart.

During this time he showed me who I was; my heart. I repented all summer long! He showed me how selfish and all of the ripple-effects of my decisions in other people's lives. I repented for everything I could ever think of! I even went to the lake in Lebanon one day and sat there for at least six hours just talking to God. Man that was such a good and intimate day! He made me write down everyone I slept with and had any soul-ties with. You don't know how hard that was! I wept. At the end of it, I held the list up to Heaven and I said, "Lord, I forgive every person on this list for hurting me. Please forgive me for every sin affected with these decisions, and I forgive MYSELF." Then I wadded up the paper and threw it in the lake. I watched as the waters overtook it and covered it and took it underneath. The Lord spoke to me and said, "This is my blood covering your sins." I cried so hard.

That is just one example. Anyways, during this time I had so much advice:

You should do it this way...

You should be doing this to get a job...doing that...

You're not doing enough...

You're too super-spiritual, get balance in your life

You're crazy

We're not going to help you because you deserve what is going to happen...

Don't ask us for help...

You've went off the deep-end...Etc.

So, because I didn't fit into their mold, they abandoned me. The whole world abandoned me! I rubbed the religious system raw. I wasn't conforming to their mold. They thought my suffering was crazy.

I don't know how to explain it except that I had to fight through the storm, through the fiery darts, through the pain, through the repentance, through the shame, through the unworthiness, through MYSELF.

The Lord told me I was marrying a pastor and I needed to leave my church to be mentored by other pastors so that they could show me the backside of the ministry. It will be training ground in ministry.

So, after losing my brand new car and then my apartment, my awesome new pastor told me that I needed to fast tomorrow. She instructed me to go to my special spot and that God had an appointment with me.

I knew what she meant. My prayer closet is the woods. I am Cherokee Indian and I found God in the woods when I was a little girl. So I feel closer to him in nature.

I love the sounds of the woods...the creek...the trees, the air I breathe, the big beautiful sky, etc. So I knew he wanted to see me in "our special spot".

I went to meet him early in the morning.

When I went to my holy place, HE MET ME THERE. I recorded it! When I go in the Holy of Holies, it is so precious. I would rather pray than breathe. I would rather be with him in that prayer closet than with my kids. He is everything to me. So, when I started talking to him I felt a sermon coming on. It was almost like giving birth. When I get in the Holy of Holies I preach most of the time.

I recorded that sermon! An hour long! After I received the sermon, I knew that my whole life...everything I've been through...all the rejection...all the hurts...all the mistakes...EVERYTHING about June Knight brought me to this point in my life. It's all about my purpose and destiny!

So, now that I am back in the prayer closet...He let me know my whole life was set for THIS...for Such a Time as This!!!

Taking My Children Back

When I first got back in the prayer closet the Lord showed me how bad off my children were in the spirit. He said, "Are your children preaching now?" I said, "No." He said, "That's right, because you've been off wollering in your sorrow and sadness and the devil's taken your children and now they haven't preached once since you've quit praying." Man did I repent like crazy. It was horrible to look at my actions and what I had done to my children!

Let me tell you, a praying momma is powerful! I can tell you stories of where I prayed for them and how God saved us. However, I will do that in another book.

To this day I'm still praying for my children to be the powerful preachers that I know they are called to be! God has given me dreams to let me know that we will all be ministering together one day!

Two Commands From God

At the beginning of the PIT experience I heard two commands from God,

1. Pray for people that are dying and
2. Use what you learned in college to help my people. I'm your boss.

Since this time I found a hospice program and started volunteering and then I started helping ministries.

We are Worthy

Early in the pit, the Lord said, "Don't be vain." I said, "What do you mean Lord?" He said, "Do you remember what you did to Rod Parsley in Bible College when he tried to get you on the platform and you refused because you were in an ugly dress?" I said, "Yes sir." He said, "I tried to put you on a world-wide stage back then and I will do it again and you better not turn it down again. You do what I say when I say it no matter what you look like." I said, "Yes sir."

Boy did He put me to the test to! One time I was about to interview this pastor on television and I was homeless so I didn't have my hair done or makeup and when I was walking up on the platform to do the show, the Holy Spirit said, "This is what I'm talking about. It's not about how you look and it's not about you. It's about the mission."

The Lord gave me a dream….

Tuesday, September 24, 2013

I saw my son Andrew Knight in a very nice suit and looking sharp. He was standing in World Harvest Church on the floor in front of where Pastor Rod Parsley (PRP) sits. Then I saw Pastor Parsley pointing to him telling him something….

Then Pastor Parsley called my name and I stood up in my rags, full of shame and embarrassed. Pastor said, go UP on the platform and stand by Joni. I said, "I can't, I don't have the clothes." PRP said, "Put on Joni's robe". I put it over my back and lowly walked on the platform. I walked past my son thinking, "He's so much more worthy than me." So when I got to the top PRP said, "Go stand by Joni." I stood beside her and was bent over like I wasn't worthy to be in this position. Pastor Parsley pointed to me and proclaimed, "I am giving you MY house and MY car."

Then I woke up.

Now, eight years later, after much battle and in the middle of a storm, the Lord gives me this dream and PRP calls me to the platform again. I felt that unworthiness again. The Lord is letting me know to accept all gifts He has for me. God tried to bless me and rise me up back in 2005. In my rags and the feeling of unworthiness, I didn't rise to occasion. Pastor Rod Parsley represents my father in Heaven (my spiritual father) and this time when he blesses me with my new house and new car (he promised me that same semester…2005)…I will accept God's gifts and not have the unworthiness attached because JESUS CLOTHED ME IN HIS BLOOD-STAINED ROBE OF RIGHTEOUSNESS (Joni's robe).

Thank you Jesus. I repented and thank the Lord he will give me a 2nd chance to accept his wonderful gifts because I am worthy. He tried to send me my promised husband years ago too and I couldn't see it because I didn't feel worthy of that man due to my past. This time I will accept ALL GIFTS.

My Love for Cheerleading

After my Conversion, the Lord really rebuked me because of my role in cheerleading in encouraging little girls to listen to that demonic, satanic music like Beyoncé, etc. I influenced thousands of girls over 13 years of coaching. I had to greatly repent!

125

This is my story of cheerleading…..

I had never cheered before; however I took dancing for many years. I assumed I would be good at cheerleading because of my personality. So, even

though I didn't know anything about it, I tried out for the high school team.

When they announced that I made the team, I could not believe it! I was so happy!

Needless to say, cheerleading changed my life. It made me believe in something. I was able to really express my personality and encourage others to be happy when in my heart I may not be happy. I loved the sport of it as well as the crowd responses.

Halfway through the season my coaches sit me down and said, "You need to hang around your own kind." I said, "What do you mean?" They said, "You need to hang around jocks." I said, "I'm sorry, I can't do that. I will be nice to anyone if they are nice to me." Due to this decision, they would not allow me to try out for the Varsity squad. I was devastated!

The school was shocked too because classmates would come up to me all the time telling me how I will make Most School Spirit. I was always making signs and was Class Representative, etc.

Then, the man my mother lived with cheated on her so we had to move back to the country! Yes…back to hickville! By this time I was a different person! I dressed different…acted different, etc. No way had I wanted to go back to Hell! Well, when we went back, I found out they were having high school try outs! I just knew I'd make that squad because I did our cheer camp at UT Knoxville and I knew how good I was. 14 girls tried out and 13 made it.

I WAS THE ONLY ONE THAT DID NOT MAKE IT! I was so shocked.

So, I asked the coach about why I didn't make it and she said, "Because of whom you USED to be. We couldn't let you be on the squad." I replied, "That was over three years ago…I'm a different person now! Please…you can't do this to me." They did.

So, after this experience my mother kicked me out of the house and then I got married at 16. So…life was headed another direction….

I Made Sure Other Girls Had a Chance with the Sport

So, when my daughter was six (6) years old, my sons were playing football and I signed her up for cheerleading. I ended up coaching her from that point all the way until she graduated. What an honor! Before she graduated high school we also were able to coach a squad together! We won championships and did all kinds of great things

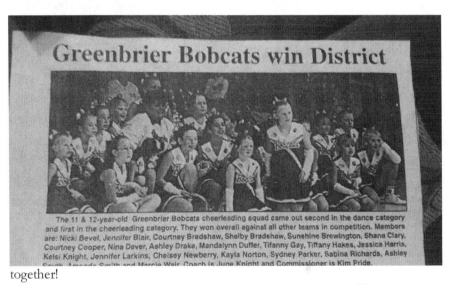

Greenbrier Bobcats win District

The 11 & 12-year-old Greenbrier Bobcats cheerleading squad came out second in the dance category and first in the cheerleading category. They won overall against all other teams in competition. Members are: Nicki Bevel, Jennifer Blair, Courtney Bradshaw, Shelby Bradshaw, Sunshine Brewington, Shana Clary, Courtney Cooper, Nina Dever, Ashley Drake, Mandalynn Duffer, Tifanny Gay, Tiffany Hakes, Jessica Harris, Kelsi Knight, Jennifer Larkins, Chelsey Newberry, Kayla Norton, Sydney Parker, Sabina Richards, Ashley South, Amanda Smith and Marcie Weir. Coach is June Knight and Commissioner is Kim Pride.

together!

The first team I coached was in Greenbrier, TN. It was awesome coaching here because her dad and I both went to school in Greenbrier. It also helped because she was cheering for her brothers. They were very good at football.

Then, in 1998 when I first started coaching her I saw that the football league's cheerleading program needed some serious help. So, I formed a

cheerleading association over 13 cities. This association is still going today. The Middle Tennessee Jr. League Cheerleaders Association (MTJLCA). I formed a partnership with Cheer Nation for the girls to advance from our competition to the national level.

I could write a book about my experience with MTJLCA...but the main point of my experience with them is the unity of the cities. When I first started coaching, none of the cities were friendly to each other. However, over the years of hard work, it broke down a lot of walls and unity became a reality.

I was able to give back to the sport when I feel like other held me back from receiving from it. I've always loved it and am very thankful for the sport of Cheerleading!

I had the honor of coaching a team with my daughter when she was a senior in high school. This is the picture above with the girls in blue. We had so much fun enjoying the sport together and encouraging other little girls.

One day my cheerleading alumni from Beech High School called me and asked me if I wanted to come back and cheer on a Friday night with my old squad.

She explained that we would be cheering with the new cheerleaders and that it would be all of the cheerleaders from the time the school started. I jumped on the opportunity. It was hard because I was the biggest cheerleader. I surely enjoyed it though!

God Made Me Repent to the World on Facebook

During my summer of repentance the Lord woke me up one morning and told me to repent to the whole world for making a mockery of His name after going to Bible College. It went something like this:

The Lord woke me up this morning and told me I must confess and repent to all my family, friends, Bible College friends, etc. I backslid after Bible College and did things I'm not proud of. I was sad over how things ended there and please forgive me for turning my back on God and hurting His name.

Well people got saved through that and most people responded saying I was forgiven.

I Preached for the First Time

A couple of months after the conversion, mom had a women's conference at her church. When I was praying about what to preach on, the Lord gave me a download and I must put this historical sermon in the next book: Please see the Clarion Call Chapter – Martyrdom in the We are the Bride Series, Volume 2: Clarion Call to Unity in God's Great Garden.

I Lost It All

At the time when I drew the line in the sand to the devil and said, "NO MORE! I'M DONE WITH YOU", I laid down my life and surrendered to God's will. Once I did that, He started waking me up again to pray, making me repent about everything and to everyone, and shut all the doors to provision again. After I caught on to what He was doing, I quickly remembered Bible College. When people were putting me down for not having a job and how I am out of God's will for not working, I would tell them, "Talk to God about it. I keep applying for jobs and He won't open the door." I got so sick of people saying that so I would cry to God about it all the time. One day God said, "I am your boss." I said, "Yes, but people don't see you paying me." He said, "Trust me."

While I'm following God's every command, I began losing everything. When they took my brand new car away, I took a picture of it and posted it on Facebook and said, "There goes my car."

Then I lost my apartment and began the process of just following God wherever He would lead me.

For the next two years I was homeless and would live in various homes. I lived with many ministers and learned from them…both good and bad. You can always learn from people. I have a servant's heart and wanted to serve all these pastors in obedience to God.

God's Promises

The Lord told me that my promises from Bible College days about the house and car are still coming to pass! He told me to let him know what kind of car I wanted. Well, I knew after driving the homeless in my new Toyota Camry that I didn't want cloth seats. I needed leather seats so I could just wipe them or spray them.

So, after much research I said I wanted a Cadillac Escalade. I needed the big vehicle to travel and minister. I also wanted a sunroof and all power with computer screen in the car. I just wanted the car loaded.

I knew God was serious and how He is about being particular and details so I wanted to make sure I answered Him in full satisfaction.

I can just hear some of you, "Why would God give her a car and house?"

Well, all I can say is that he woke me up one morning in Bible College and told me, "Because you gave up your house and car for me, I will bless you with so much more than you could ever dream of." So, he promised me and I'm still waiting on it to come to pass and I fully expect it.

The Water in My Hell

Unless you've been without a job, homeless and haven't had money in a long time, then you may not understand the joy of just thinking of working and making money. People act like everyone just wants to be lazy and not work, when it may be that God has them in that position for training, purging and sifting. Many preachers call it the "process" meaning when people are in their deserts or pits. It means that everything is out of control and the person is forced to be on a limb with nothing but faith to hold on to for survival.

So, during the first summer when I was so desperate for money and a job, I had a pastor friend in Lebanon offer me a job.

I drove out there and the church said, "We will give you a job at the church to help with the Thrift Store and you can help us with marketing and advertising.

We will give you a place to live for free until you get on your feet. We would love to have you join our church; we need your help!" Awe man, I was so excited! I was thinking, "Yes Lord! Woohoo! Move to a town where the church actually wants me to get involved! In a city where the people love me and don't judge me by my past? A fresh start? A new life? An awesome pastor? Yes Lord!"

So next night we're having a prayer meeting with his church and the anointing is so thick in the room and he says, "June, I hate to tell you this more than anything, but the Lord said to tell you that we cannot hire you or move you here. You have to go back to Clarksville! I'm so sorry." I started crying like a baby! I have to go back to the desert!

I have to go back to the church that has deserted me 10 years ago and don't want me there. I have to go back to the community where I've been in every bar in my past and have made such a mockery of God's name! I have to go back to the city where they all knew I failed in Bible College! Noooo!

The pastor grabs the Israel prayer shawl and puts it over my head and anointed me with oil. He said, "This night the Lord ordains you to be the physical representation of the Bride of Christ." He then prayed for me strength to go back to the Hell.

The Soul-Tie Deliverance at the River

I'm sitting at the river crying about going back to Clarksville where I feel so rejected and alone and the Lord starts dealing with me about soul-ties. He said, "I want you to write down every person you've slept with." I said, "Oh Lord, what if I can't remember them all." He said, "Just write down what you remember about them or the place."

So I started writing them down and when I started realizing what I had done to my temple and how I had let all these people take advantage of this temple and how I had no respect for my temple, I cried like a baby. I couldn't believe what I saw when I faced God in the throne room about my sex life. I was a sex addict and had abused my body.

I realized how Satan had attacked me since a little girl to defile this temple.

131

I spent six hours with the Lord that day groaning and repenting in intercession. When you truly repent about something you face yourself in a mirror. I didn't like what I saw. Who is this woman that would allow herself to be sold?

Who is this woman that would allow her children to see her with different boyfriends all the time? Who is this woman that would just marry men for security? This woman had an offer one time to be on a pornography movie and even considered it because it was such great money. How low this temple got to even consider such a thing. So many things I had done that I suddenly became ashamed of. I considered how I sold my body to the highest bidder. Just gross before a heavenly God.

So, I held the list up to Heaven at the end of the repentance and said, "God, I forgive every person on this list and even the ones I can't remember, and please forgive ME for everything I did to hurt these people!

I pray right now you release me from these soul ties never to be there again! I am free in Jesus' name!" So I crumbled the list up and threw it in the river.

The cutest little wave came up and covered the list and sunk it to the bottom and the Holy Spirit said, "That is my blood covering your sins." I cried so hard. I could hardly breathe!

Now that I'm traveling and preaching, I see why God did that. Now I can stand before thousands and say, "If God can take an old whore like I was, a woman at the well and make her pure, THEN HE CAN MAKE ANY ONE OF YOU PURE!" So, they line up from one side of the church to the other...the young and the old. People are just bound up with impurities. God wants to make his bride pure.

Now Pray for Your Pastor

Well I hear you asking, "What happened to your pastor?" Well, since Bible College he wouldn't look at me anymore or allow me to get near him. His assistant pastor would always block us from talking. I tried so many times to ask him to forgive me. I sent a card home one time through his mother. No answer. I tried calling the church. No answer. I tried going through the assistant pastor. No answer. So, God wouldn't let me leave the church either.

I felt much rejected in that church. I believe it was because the pastor rejected me. It's probably because the church thought I was a wishy-washy person too. I don't know. It's just the point that it was a very strained relationship since I returned from Bible College.

My son Andrew got married while in Bible College and also also acquired a position at World Harvest Church so he is still there. When we returned back to Tennessee it was just me and Meagan.

We lived so many different places trying to survive so I was in and out of the church as well. Plus, I lived with my old partying buddy for a while and got back in the partying scene as well. I was just miserable all the way around.

Now, here's the thing I must say about the church and the bar friends. Man was I loved in the partying scene. I sure wasn't rejected there! They loved my personality, I got to sing karaoke, and dance (remember I love dancing), and laugh. When I'd go to church I felt so rejected and judged. I felt unworthy to be there.

Now I'm sure that the pastor knew I was living a double-standard life as well so he was probably ashamed of me over that as well. Either way it goes, we never talked again.

So, when I had the Saul conversion, about three months later the Lord says, "I want you to start praying for your pastor like you do your children." I said, "OK Lord." I knew these prayers were different. It was serious intercession.

So, I go down to the prayer closet in the woods and I start out by saying the normal prayers, "Lord I bless his ministry, bless him, etc." After a little bit of praying in tongues in intercession, the Lord took me to the throne room. He showed me like a video screen what really happened 10 years ago with this pastor. I was horrified! I didn't realize I hurt this man and his ministry so much. I cried so hard I could hardly breathe. I repented with my whole heart. It was like it was at the lake when He showed my life in the mirror with other men. He showed me in a mirror what I did to not only this man but the whole ministry.

When God shows you how you affected a person, their ministry and a whole city...you are either going to repent or run. I repented. When I finished seeing all the things that were the truth, I began to prophesy and declare with such boldness for him to be restored in every way that the devil had stolen from him through me!

I prayed he would meet a woman that is so much better than I could have ever been, grant him a son, even in his older age, restore his youth like the eagles, restore his visions, community, etc. I was violent with it too! I knew that since by MY actions that I had practically destroyed this man that by the same person I was going to fight with all I could to reverse the curse! I was telling that devil where to go! I was begging God to restore him.

I went back to the church and told him that I was praying for him and how sorry I was that I wasn't praying for him like I should. Since I had the Saul conversion things at the church have been getting better. God sent me one friend there that I just love. She stuck by me this past year and a half through the PIT. This family has supported me through it all and I'm very thankful!

The pastor pulled me aside one day after church this year and said, "Just to let you know, all is well and all is forgiven." So I'm thankful that's all over.

Right after that confrontation in prayer in the woods about my pastor, God told me I was no longer going to be at that church because I was going to marry a pastor and had to leave this church to serve another ministry to learn the backside of a ministry. This is the first time God told me to leave this church.

Move in With Woman Preacher

The next week after God tells me to leave that old church I move in with this woman. Wow, this family is like a dream family. The woman is a preacher with a very supportive husband and children. She has four children, one was grown and she home-schooled the other three. She was the full-time pastor of a church and an international ministry.

She began mentoring me on ministry and showing me the backside of the ministry. I learned so much about how things are ran behind the scenes and why pastors do some of the things they do. She would sit me down in the mornings and challenge me to do things that would rub my flesh so raw but I would do them in obedience. She treated me just like a true mentor would. God had spoken to her about my challenges and she set to break those things off me. Yes, it hurt my flesh, but I submitted.

I cried so much living with her because God was burning so many things out of me. I learned just as much by watching her with her family.

What a servant she was to her whole house. She would serve her children and when her husband was at home she served him like a king. She instructed her children that when he comes home for one hour for lunch (he was a business man), for them to be quiet and let him talk because he was the man of the house and it was his only time during the day to talk.

Man that was so different than how I was raised! I never had a dad or a good role model as a man in my life so I had to be so strong-willed that he wouldn't be top priority like this. Anyways, after living with her I realize so many things I did wrong with the kid's dad and wished I would have known then. I realized that I didn't respect him enough as the man and the breadwinner of the house. This is probably one reason why he was always so angry.

Who knows why he did what he did, but I'm not blaming it all on him. I know I had issues too and living with this woman caused me to examine my heart on being a woman with a man and future pastor husband.

So, one of the gifts she gave me when I left was a book about how to love a man. I can't remember the name of it but it was about keeping him as the King of the house.

My Prophetic Wedding to Jesus

When I moved in with this woman the Lord told me to tell her everything so after I told her about marrying the Lord in baptism she suggested we do a wedding to publicly marry Him since my ministry will be "We are the Bride". So we planned this big wedding, did a press release and invited the community and public. WOMAN MARRIES JESUS.

So, my family attends and I felt like a Queen before my King.

His presence was all over me! I knew it was the first Bridefest ceremony. The Lord even gave me the vows in the prayer closet.

October 27, 2013

God Gave Me a Car!

After six months of going without a car, my brother and sister-in-law called me and said that they were going to bless me with their son's old car. They told me that the check engine light was on and it had an oil leak but I could have it as long as it's still running. It's a 2000 Toyota Camry.

I was so happy to have this car! Even if it was just a short amount of time! AT LEAST IT RAN!!

It had like 215,000 miles on it! But the air conditioning worked, etc. I also loved the sunroof.

2000 Toyota Camry, Blessing from my family; Bobby and Tammy. Thank you!

136

Holy Spirit Always Warns Me

At this time I was living with a stranger in Clarksville. I was homeless and put an ad on Craigslist to ask someone to take me in and I would help them with their website, etc. This man answered my ad and said he had an extra room. He said he worked all the time and rents that room out but he wouldn't charge me if I would keep his house clean because he doesn't have time. I knew I was doing ministry in Clarksville and he had internet so it worked out good for both of us.

Well one night he was at the bar and I had a dream. I saw this man at the end of my bed and he crawled under the covers to rape me. I said, "What are you doing?" He said, "You know you want it." So, I woke up rebuking the devil and he came home about five minutes later. I was so thankful because the Holy Spirit always warns me and I can pray against attacks.

I began praying and declaring against that attack. He never touched me or tried anything. I just stayed in my room and minded my own business. At the end however he did start mocking me and putting me down and eventually God opened the door for me to move somewhere else.

God sent the Army

This dream was on March 18, 2014

So, while I was there I had another dream:

Rarely do I have dreams where I feel in the physical as I'm dreaming. However, in this case I did. I was lying in the bed and all of a sudden I felt this fire in the pit of my stomach. I know some preachers have described this as "fire shut up in my bones" or "I feel the FIRE on the inside of me". Well I was thinking, "I feel a great expectancy!

Something great is about to happen." It was a feeling of excitement in the air…expectancy. Then came the dream…

I was lying on dirt in the middle of the desert. The wind was blowing over my hair but I had passed out from exhaustion and thirst. My lips were chapped, skin dehydrated, and my clothes were raggedy and dirty. I looked wore out like I couldn't go another step.

Then all of a sudden the ground starts shaking. I feel my body move from the violence of it. I hear horses' hooves like a great army of horses running.

I hear like a shofar blowing so I rise up with the last bit of energy I have to see what it is. I could hardly see through the cloud of dust then they all come to a stop in front of me. It was an army on chariots like you see in movies. They were in a semi-circle around me. To the left I could see men on chariots of gold like as far as I could see. Then I looked to the right and same thing. These men had armor on from head to toe like they were ready to fight a battle. They had bow and arrows and long spears of gold.

Then I looked in front and there was a man in a white robe glowing on the chariot directly in front of me. His chariot was different. Gold and massive. His horses were white…pearly white. The horses were so majestic-looking and stood at attention like they were on a mission.

He exited his chariot and walked towards me. It was odd because when He put his foot on the dirt, there was complete silence! You could hear a pin drop!

He walked towards me and as He got closer I knew it was Jesus…the one I've been praying to! The closer He got the more love I felt. I felt restoration pouring into my weak, worn out body. I could feel the love rushing through my bones.

I could literally feel the restoration coming to my cells, etc. When he stood in front of me, he reached down with his hand to pick me up; it was like salvation all over again! It was like slow motion of my answer arriving! When He touched my hand and pulled me up, it was such love, grace and mercy flowing over me. I could feel it. Restoration IN EVERY PART OF MY BEING. It was like my cells were even reacting to His presence. I could feel my skin turning young and youthful again. Everything was being healed!

As Jesus was pulling me up He said, "My child, you will never lack again. Now, rise up and help my people. You were born for such a time as this." When I stood before him, I looked down and my raggedy garments had changed to a royal gown of gold. I looked totally different! My hair was styled beautifully and I just looked like a queen of royal magnitude! A tiara came down from Heaven and fell on my head.

I looked behind the front of the chariots and I couldn't believe what I saw!

I COULDN'T BELIEVE IT! There were chariots as far as I could see full of barrels of oil! OIL! I was like, "Jesus, what are those? What are they for?" He said, "Help my people." Then he was raptured out. He rose straight up and left me!

HE LEFT THE ARMY! The army looked at me like I was their commander now. I was thinking, "What do I do with this Army?" Then all of a sudden they all moved beside me. To the left the chariots lined up in precise order and rolled their chariots behind me. To the right…the chariots did the same. AS FAR AS I COULD SEE!

Then, all the other chariots of oil were behind me! I looked to the left and saw the sergeants of the Army looking at me in unison like I was the leader. Then I looked to the right and they did the same thing. The army was waiting for me to say CHARGE! So, I leaned back like I was throwing a softball and yelled as loud as I could, CHARRRGGGGGGGGGGGGGEEEEEE! AND THREW MY HAND FORWARD…Then I woke up.

This dream was so weird because I woke up homeless basically, in my pit, abandoned by everyone and all alone. I'm like, How can I lead an army?

Satan Visited Me

About six months after the Army dream, I was actually homeless on the streets. All the other days I was homeless but living with other people and some I didn't know. However, this one night I was homeless in my car.

It was on a Saturday night and I found a place to sleep. It was a hot August night and I was all sweating in the car.

It definitely gave me insight into how homeless people hate going to church. Even just one night on the streets was causing me to consider not going. I couldn't fix my hair, I was afraid I would be stinking, etc.

Anyway, the next morning I was underneath an awning at an old business killing time and I was standing outside my car praising God. It was storming so bad you could hardly see. All of a sudden this red silhouette of a man comes walking through the rain storm. He walked up to me and said, "Why don't you just quit. Everyone thinks you're crazy because you are. Here you are with a Master's degree and you're homeless! You thought you were all that and you're nothing. Just give up. Everyone is against you for a reason. YOU are the one that is crazy, not them!" So at first I listened because I was pretty depressed and then I came to my senses and said, "Satan, you have no right to be talking to me because I have not opened the door to you. I rebuke you!" So, he left.

I went to church in that condition and just lay on the floor weeping before the Lord. I just couldn't go another step unless He gave me more grace. So that night a woman came up to me in my other church and said, "The Lord told me to have you live with me until the first of the year for free." So, I moved in with her that night then God called me out for a season.

Many Dreams

I've had many dreams over the past two years. This is a dream I had about a butterfly:

The Butterfly on a Tree Dream:

I was a butterfly hanging on a tree. I knew it was my time to fly.so I let go of the tree and was flying through the beautiful field of flowers then crossed over the hill into a beautiful field of wheat. There was MILLIONS of wheat!

I stopped in the middle of that field and my butterfly GREW AS BIG AS THE WHEAT! I hovered over the millions...my wings spanned out as far as they reached...all the way around!

Then the sun shined from Heaven and shined right through the butterfly! The iridescent colors just glistened on the wheat! So many different colors and sparkles! It was so bright and beautiful!

Then...the wheat starts clapping their hands! They were in awe of the rays of beauty from the sun! They all stood there clapping in amazement.

Then, next thing you know, God's hand as big as the sky come down and swiped up the butterfly and took it to Heaven with him!

The dream about a Fruit Tree:

I had a dream that I was in my new house and I was standing on my back deck looking into the back yard. There was a beautiful tree right in the middle that had all different types of fruit growing from it. I mean it had bananas, apples, oranges and different fruits. I ran out the back porch to eat one fruit. As I ate it, the tree automatically grew another one. So, I kept eating and it kept growing.

I saw like the house full of people and they were looking at this tree in amazement. I was like what kind do you want and it would just grow it. I would tell the tree what I needed and it would be there.

Then the tree kept growing taller and thicker and it grew up through the clouds. When I needed a fruit, I would holler and tell it what I needed and with ease it would bend down and give it to me! It was very apparent to the guests how blessed I am with all this fruit! As much as I would get, I would GIVE IT. I kept hearing, FRUIT THAT WILL REMAIN. FRUIT THAT WILL REMAIN."

Scriptures God gave me that night:

John 15:16 - You did not choose Me but I chose you, and appointed you that you would go and bear fruit, and that your fruit would remain, so that whatever you ask of the Father in My name He may give to you.

John 15 (ESV) I Am the True Vine

15 "I am the true vine, and my Father is the vinedresser. 2 Every branch in me that does not bear fruit he takes away, and every branch that does bear fruit he prunes, that it may bear more fruit. 3 Already you are clean because of the word that I have spoken to you. 4 Abide in me, and I in you. As the branch cannot bear fruit by itself, unless it abides in the vine, neither can you, unless you abide in me. 5 I am the vine; you are the branches. Whoever abides in me and I in him, he it is that bears much fruit, for apart from me you can do nothing. 6 If anyone does not abide in me he is thrown away like a branch and withers;

and the branches are gathered, thrown into the fire, and burned. 7 If you abide in me, and my words abide in you, ask whatever you wish, and it will be done for you. 8 By this my Father is glorified, that you bear much fruit and so prove to be my disciples. 9 As the Father has loved me, so have I loved you. Abide in my love. 10 If you keep my commandments, you will abide in my love, just as I have kept my Father's commandments and abide in his love. 11 These things I have spoken to you, that my joy may be in you, and that your joy may be full.

The fruit looked so big colorful and juicy. The tree kept growing taller but when I needed a fruit it would bend down so I could pick it off with such ease! There were many people going in and out of that house and I was blessing them with this fruit. It was obvious and apparent to them how blessed I was. The tree was so big and fluffy.

9
EXPERIENCES IN MINISTRY DURING PIT

Ministering to the Elderly

My Moment with Benjamin

Once upon a Time

A man lived on Earth who was so sublime

His name is Benjamin...I will never forget

My Moment with Benjamin

They called me to come pray

During his last moments on Earth

Oh, my moment with Benjamin

The Royalty God revealed about Him

The moment I touched him

The Lord opened the portal into Heaven

To see his entrance

I saw the angels, family members, and all the hosts of Heaven

Bowed down to greet him

As he met the one he served

I could not pray but weep

At the Royal Moment of Time

Benjamin was a humble man

On Earth for 101 years, married to His lovely wife 73 years

Served his church for 75 years

And the last 40 years of his life...

He served the Body of Christ

By just cleaning his church after the services

Not looking for Praise on Earth

But, Oh the Royalty I saw.......Just because He Served

**The Lord woke me up a couple of months later and gave me a song and
it's called ROYAL MOMENT OF TIME**

My Moment with the 110 Year-Old

I ministered to her for last six months of her life
It was mostly filled with no strife
She was a beautiful African-American
I'm sure a Good Samaritan!
She was a jolly 'ole soul
Up until recently she was very active and life did not take its toll
She told me how her family was so blessed
As her 91 year-old daughter took care of her even while she digressed
She always made me smile
As I held her hand and prayed for her a long while
She made it on the news as the oldest citizen in Tennessee
Then the Lord took her four days later to be with Him you see

My Moment with So-Called Crazy Lady

When I met this woman they called schizophrenic crazy lady
It didn't take long to see they misunderstood her
Because she was a Pentecostal Brady
We became very close in those four months
As she told stories of missing her pastor from 30 years prior
I found him and informed him of her last wishes and desire
He quickly came and I saw her face light up like a candle
I took pictures of the two and for her to handle
We prayed often about the children's lack of visitation
Asking God to grant her wish of their visit with no hesitation
One day they called to repossess my car and I only had one hour
I went to see my friend to inform her and saw God's power
For she was in a coma her last day on Earth
And God brought her out to say "I love you" and it had worth
The Lord took her home that night
And woke her children up to be with her as she took that flight.
I'll miss my friend of labels of crazy
As I know in my heart she was a beautiful daisy.

An Elderly Miracle

A friend asked me to visit her mother

She was bound to her chair and face frozen from a stroke of another

I told her I was sent by her daughter to pray for her

As I begin to pray and pour out my heart, the Holy Spirit began to defer

She rose up from the chair, with all sobriety

And said, "Now let's pray for your sister", with all piety

She leaned back in her chair in her frozen state

My mouth to the floor in awe of this fate

For at the time my sister claimed Atheist in her heart

So this was God's way of showing me how He is ready to impart

God will watch over my family

As I serve Him wherever He sends in anomaly

What the Lord Revealed to Me About the Elderly

Our society has lost respect for the elderly. We forget they were the ones who made this nation so great. We also forget what the bible says about respecting and honoring the elderly.

Our society and culture also says beauty is young smooth skin, very petite women, and wearing clothing that is revealing. Well, one day I was touching the 109 year-old lady I was visiting on her face. I was noticing the wrinkles and the black spots on her face. I also noticed the lack of hair, etc. The Lord spoke to me, "I love her face. I see her beauty where the world does not. Her face is like the rings on a tree. It tells a story of the years of her life."

After that experience I told the Lord that I want to visit all the nations of the Earth and I want to touch their faces too. God revealed to me that all the different types of faces are Him. He's so big and vast that He is made up of variety. The people that try to put him in a box are missing out on how great our God is. He's every color. He's every face. We are all him.

Another thing I learned is how the spirit works. I prayed with many people in comas knowing that they can hear me inside. They are very much alive in there although their bodies have failed them. So, talk to them knowing they hear you.

I had a guy on the radio one time that was in a 40-day coma. He said that during this time he was floating down a river of lava headed to Hell. People in the world just thought he was in a coma, but the reality was that he was that close to Hell. He said he could hear people screaming as they were being tortured by demons, etc. All of a sudden they were about to go off a cliff and he knew it was the point of no return so he cried out to God to be saved and a branch appeared and he pulled himself out of the river and woke up out of the coma screaming, "I WANT TO GET SAVED NOW! SAVE ME GOD! SAVE ME!" So, yes, they are alive and talk to them.

I also realized how sad our churches were because there are so many people in nursing homes and no one visits them. Please, if you're hungry and looking for somewhere to minister, preach, or just love on people, go to your local nursing home. You'd be surprised at the stories the elderly can tell you. It's a great ministry!

Prison Ministry

I love the prison ministry more than any other type! They are so hungry and you have to be a real Christian or they will spit you out.

Currently I minister in two states Tennessee and Kentucky. I minister in both the men's and women's prisons. However, I really prefer the men's prison because they're more expressive and responsive for some reason.

A minister really needs the gifts of the Holy Spirit to minister in prisons. I'll give you an example:

One day I was in a women's prison and I was the scheduled speaker. The women that come in were cold as ice. They were not paying attention and talking during the worship. So, I began praying in tongues and asking the Holy Spirit how He wanted me to preach. He gave me a word.

So, I go up to the platform and they were still in their own world and I said, "I was over there praying in the spirit and the Lord gave me a word for someone…" I released that word and it was like BAM! It cut through that hardness like a knife! I mean they all stopped talking and paid attention the rest of the night. They were glued to what I had to say because they knew God was in the room.

Most of my sermons come through dreams. The dreams I had before prisons were the ones about love and forgiveness and the faces of God.

The sad thing about prison ministry is that you only have about five minutes to pray with each prisoner so you're very careful about what you pray because it must be exact and precise!

Also, when I preach in the prisons about the trees and how each tree is unique to God and specifically designed by Him…it helps them a lot!

Servanthood to Ministers

The Out-of-State Disaster

After serving ministries for a year in my state and serving them, God gave me a dream and He said, "You are going to serve one more ministry before I launch your ministry. This ministry is out of state. The only thing I ask is that you keep your mouth shut." I thought this was a weird instruction but I was excited that I was going to serve another ministry! I had been serving many ministries over the past year. God gave me a dream the year before about unity in our city so I go to the mayor and the city spiritual leaders and try to obey the Lord and it became a disaster because the pastors would not come together in unity. They would when it was their church being highlights but when it came to advertising for another church they wouldn't do it. So, needless to say that vision of unity flopped. I tried.

However, now that I knew I was going somewhere out of town I was so excited! It took about a month before that ministry called, but when they did I was so excited! It was a woman who had been ministering in our town before and she knew the lady I lived with previously and other ministers. Well she called me and told me that God told her to let me come live with her to help her with her media ministry. She needed help doing websites, etc. So, the plan was to come for three months (until January), and help her ministry. To get everything done that she wanted, it would take all of that time.

Well I was highly favored in her eyes until one day her interactions with me on the phone changed to more of anger and cynicism towards me. She began putting me down about my old car that I drove, etc. She said, "Don't you realize how pastors make fun of you for the car you drive?" I said, "Well they can talk to God about it because he gave me that car."

I knew someone or people had called her and trashed me. I kind of had an idea of who the person is. I hated it because we had a great relationship.

Anyways, this woman begins to tell me, "You are going to come up here and serve me and you must be self-sufficient. You must pay your gas and way up here, supply your food, and take care of your way home. I don't have enough money to take care of you too while you're up here." So I told her, "If God wants me up there He will take care of me." I also told her I had food stamps so I should be fine on the food part.

However, I knew I would have to trust God for the gas money and that the car would even make it there.

The car began making popping noises like it was about to fall apart. So, this woman kept telling me she didn't think that car would take me there.

To make a long story short, she was so negative before I even came, and then shortened the trip to three weeks because of what that other person said.

On my way there on nothing but faith and a full tank of gas, the car

sounded like it was about to fall apart. It was barely creeping down the interstate like 40 miles per hour and jerking real bad. I got so mad and started beating on the dash screaming, "You will line up to the will of the Living God in the name of Jesus! You will get me to to this state and back to obey God!" IMMEDIATELY the check-engine light came off in the car. The jerking quit and the car straightened up! It started driving like a charm! It

drove me like a Cadillac the whole trip!

Here's a picture of this awesome car!

I arrive at her house and she comes out and says, "I can't believe that car made it here!" I said, "Oh yes, totally by faith!" So, the whole time I was there I had this shooting pain from the bottom of my neck all the way down my right arm. It almost paralyzed that arm. I don't' know what that was. However, it was hard to work.

The reason God told me to keep my mouth shut is because she put me down the whole time I was there. Her mouth was a constant attack against me! She worked me from sun up to sun down too. She took full advantage of the time! She would say stuff like, "Do you realize how fat you are? Your hair is too big. Your makeup is wrong. Your jewelry is too trashy and gaudy.

You need to be a lady. Your clothes are wrong. You're not putting THAT stuff in my house where people can see it.

You will be in the back bedroom where no one can see your stuff." It was stuff like that all the time. I tried so hard to keep my mouth shut but I failed when she said this, "Don't you realize you can break furniture being that big?" I looked at her and said, "I forgive you." She acted all innocent and said, "What? What did I do?"

(She would do that trying to act all innocent after she stabs you real good with her mouth). I said, "Don't you realize how offense that can be to a person that is not strong like I am? You could destroy a person talking to them like this." So, I had to really pray at night for God to keep my cool and my flesh to stay under control every day.

When I got there she did have a bunch of food so she did take care of the food, however she rationed it to put me on a diet. This is fine, but I wonder her motives behind it too. One day she said, "Breakfast is ready." Then she walks in her office. I walk in the kitchen and there's a boiled egg on the plate. I just sat there and prayed and thanked the Lord for my food and calmly went back to my room. (I've learned through the PIT that I cannot control what others do TO me, but I DO have to answer to God on how I handle that offense). I knew God was watching me and it was a test.

She come in there, "Well, did you enjoy your breakfast?" I said, "Yes, thank you very much." She said, "I'm surprised you're not angry it was just a boiled egg." I said, "No, thank you very much for breakfast."

So, she goes in the office and yells back in the room to me, "I told Joe Blow (I'll keep him anonymous because he's a mutual friend), that when you came here you were eating four pieces of turkey bacon, three eggs and biscuits and gravy and I've reduced you to a boiled egg."

Man my claws was coming out. My flesh wanted to deck her! I said, "I can't believe you told a man what I used to eat! Why would you tell a man anything about me personally?" That made me so mad!

Another example is that she was sitting in the room next to me working on computer and I was in the bedroom in the back working and I receive a notice from Facebook that this woman reported me to them. It was a warning. I yelled in there, "Why did you report me to Facebook?" She replied, "I want you to take that picture down."

I said, "Well, why didn't you just yell in here and tell me instead of reporting me?" She said she didn't know. It was stuff like this all the time. It was a constant test of my flesh.

See this woman was a beauty queen. She's very tiny and petite. She would come in the room and say, "Which blouse should I wear?" I would suggest one and she'd say, "OK, I'll wear the other one." Then she'd say, "Oh, if I was just younger, if I was just prettier, if I could just get a facelift." One day I told her, "The Lord told me not to be vain."

She would take two hours to get dressed and refused to go to church because she didn't have enough time to get dressed. She replied, "What do you mean vain?" I said, "He told me to go wherever He told me to go no matter what I looked like or was wearing." I was saying it because with her as a mentor I wanted her wisdom on it. She said, "He didn't tell me that."

So, I left there after three weeks and I told her all I wanted was for her to put a post on Facebook telling all the pastors back home that I treated her with honor and represented my peoples well. She said she would but when I left she wouldn't do it. She did bless me with $200 when I left. However, I wanted the good report to my pastors back home more than the money.

She also took me clothes shopping but it was because she didn't want to be seen with me in the clothing I currently had.

However, to other people, she made it look like she was buying me a bunch of clothes. She spent about $150 and made a smart remark, "I believe I'm paying you plenty for the work you did here."

I said, "Well the last job I made $800 a week so I feel like I've blessed you well too." I wanted her to know that my time was valuable as well. I don't' know, I guess I got tired of the put-downs as well and the sanctimonious looks she would give me about my size and the person I was.

When I left there I had to cast off the spirit of suicide that tried to attach itself to me there. I cast off any condemnation and it took me months to get those evil comments out of my system. It depressed me for a long time. It was every day.

It really hurt my feelings when I come back and the pastors didn't ask me how it went with her. If I sent a pastor to serve another pastor I would want to know how they treated me and if they mistreated my people, I'd have to let them know how inappropriate that was.

But, they didn't, so I just cried about it to the Lord and then I realized one day why God sent me there.

He was preparing me for the future where I will have the media and different ones coming after me and I must be able to control my tongue.

Update on my Children

All my children have one son each. I have three grandsons. My daughter ended up marrying a guy from high school who loves her dearly and they are wonderful parents of my beautiful grandson. Andrew met his beautiful wife in Bible College and they still live in Ohio. Brock is divorced and lives in Alabama. I hardly get to see my family anymore, but I sure treasure the time we have together.

Also, it was awesome knowing that all three of us was in Bible College together. Brock, Andrew and I we also do the same type of work; graphic design, videos, web design, etc.

I'm very proud of my children and they're all great parents. This means a lot to me as a mother knowing that their children will have a better future.

10
WATB MINISTRIES IS BORN

My First Book

Well after that experience out of state, God told me to take my research paper that I made a 100 on in Grad School and turn it into a book. It is called, Selling the Mark of the Beast, and can be found at www.gotreehouse.org. I released it in January 2015. This book is about how Europe and the United States are selling the RFID (Radio Frequency Identification Device) tags to humans and inserting them inside their bodies. This book brings clarity to the enemy's tactics in the last days through media, drones, etc.

Businesses

This birthed Treehouse Publishers. I then started Visions Communications for the websites, graphic design, advertising, etc.

We Are The Bride Ministries

In combination to all this WATB was born. I started out in radio and recently branched off into television. I'm waiting on God's timing for the manifestation of it all.

We are the Bride Ministries was first conceived in Bible College in the throne room and when Rod Parsley walked in and preached about it.

Then when I finally had the conversion, the pregnancy began. It was born in January 2015 with WATB Radio. Five months later I'm driving down the interstate in Alabama headed to a Women's Conference in Florida and the spirit of the Lord came in my car and I began birthing as I'm driving down the road. I'm in deep intercession with groaning's during prayer.

It's hard to explain unless you're an intercessor, you know how birthing is. It's like you're having a baby but in the spirit.

So I prayed and gave birth to this ministry driving down the interstate for three hours!

Following that encounter with God, He sent me on the road on a summer tour across the nation to kick off www.watb.tv. The summer tour was awesome. I was able to meet ministers from everywhere!

Well, God promised us a building in Nashville, TN, before I left on the trip. The staff went to the location that God promised and laid hands on the radio station and the land that God promised. God actually gave me a dream and told me to go back and declare the land for sale for the Bride.

Colossians 3:3 - For you died to this life, and your real life is hidden with Christ in God.

He told me, "Don't ask for small when it comes to my Bride! Ask for it all!" So we went back and asked for it all!

Then I got to Texas and a prophet called me and said, "God told me He's giving you a building." I said, "Yes". They said, "He told me to give you this Smith Wigglesworth book and for you to bury it on the land symbolically." So I met her in Texas and she gave the book to me in a formal presentation. Since that time I took the book and had people sign it all over the nation and the world. They are all coming in agreement that God is giving the Bride a new media.

In my heart I believe God is rising up a pure, unadulterated media. Not like TBN and other ones where it's all preaching, but full networks. So, I see all forms of communications for the Bride coming in this building!

Please pray for us. Our goal is to help the Bride effectively communicate their message to the world so that we can gather the harvest!

I believe God has called each one of us to a mission and we desire to help others to achieve their destiny through communications.

Thank you for your prayers and support.

Various Logos/Ads this Year

Finishing My Education

When God told me "NO" to the doctorate at my secular college, I had no idea it was because He wanted to bless me with a Doctorate of Christian Theology. So, a year-and-a-half into the pit, this opportunity came open. God gave me a dream that He was going to pay for it and He did!

International Miracle Institute

I attended school here for a year and graduated in August 2015 with my Doctorate in Christian Theology. I also graduated as a Founder in the First Century Faith Class. I have truly enjoyed the classes by Dr. Harfouche and his whole family! They're all highly anointed and gifted!

What I see in the Future for Me

Well now I've started the radio and television through We are the Bride Ministries and God has promised us a building, so we are in the beginning stages of achieving the full destiny that God has lined up for me.

When I started the radio station almost nine months ago, we have interviewed over 150 ministries and our intro song is like charging an army. I say, **"Go Bride! Our soon-coming king awaits!"** I feel like I'm the Bride's cheerleader now!

I do know that I will be married in the future and I can't wait to see what God does with my life with Him as my husband and leading me all the way.

HERE ARE PICTURES OF THE BRIDE COMING IN AGREEMENT WITH ME FOR A BUILDING FOR THIS MEDIA MINISTRY

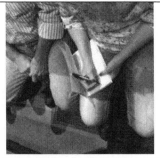

Many states and countries have signed this book: Mississippi, Louisiana, Tennessee, Alabama, New Jersey, New York, Maine, Rhode Island, California, Colorado, North Carolina, South Carolina, Georgia, Oklahoma, Nigeria, Liberia, Sierra Leone, West Africa, Kenya, Australia, Lebanon, Alaska, Canada, and many more!

This book will be buried on the land and when God provides, we will resurrect the book and enclose in a glass case to show the world how the Bride come together in agreement to take the media mountain back!

I don't know what my future holds, but I know who holds my future. I live to please Him and not man. I am currently still homeless and driving my 2000 Toyota Camry, trying to do these ministries on my own and businesses, but I know that my provision and help is coming! I do have a wonderful board that believes in me and I am so grateful! I am not looking back! I'm moving forward in full faith that God hasn't given up on me and we will finish the plan that He wrote for me before time began!

11
WISDOM GAINED FROM PIT FOR BRIDE

Not to accept offense and forgive those people IMMEDIATELY because now I KNOW who I serve and he will defend me. I pray for those people because they know not what they are doing. He is my husband and he IS HOLY!

How to recognize God's love through my shame, guilt, unworthiness, hurts, pains, sadness, loneliness, etc.

My IDENTITY - This is the most important part because now I'm pure. Who the Lamb of God is that WAS SLAIN FOR ME! I cry when I think about Him because he was so innocent and I put those nails in!

How I'm married to the holiest man on the planet – Jesus Christ!

How HOLY he really is - I fear Him more than I ever have in my life!

How he's my provider - Now that I look back...when he wanted me to pray for dying people...he kept me in a brand new car. I stayed in a brand new apartment. He kept me classy! Always gave me gas money when I needed it!

How he's my lover - He intensified my worship and prayer. He knows I'm very passionate so he shut every door to a job so that I am forced to face Him and spend time with Him. The more I spent time with Him the more he revealed Himself and revealed his passion for me as well.

How to trust HIM above everyone! He taught me that the whole world will fail me but HE NEVER WILL! He later told me that HE hardened people's hearts so that I would learn that lesson and he could reveal more about His love towards me. He's so awesome!

He showed me how HE sees the poor and the needy. It's really sad. I have SO MUCH compassion! He woke me up one morning to tell me that he's preparing me to be the Proverbs 31 woman and she loves the poor and needy!

He taught me to not question Him. Now I know that HIS PLAN IS MUCH BETTER THAN MY PLAN! The devil kept telling me I was going to be homeless because no one would help me.

He's a liar and look what God has done in the two-year PIT! He always gave me a place to sleep, food, etc. I was homeless on the streets one night.

He taught me that He can be my Husband in TN like he was in OH and I can have my Queen Hood back! I've always called Ohio my Queen Hood because when I was in Bible College it was like living on another planet. It was SO AMAZING! God paid all my bills; people would just walk up to me and hand me $1,000 dollars...go to landlord and pay rent, etc. I was his bride and he showered me with gifts, love, etc. He just let me know if I will fall back in his arms and trust him that he will be with me WHEREVER I go!

He taught me to love others even when I am hurting and need love. It's like reaping and sewing. An example of this is when they were repossessing my car, the Lord told me to go visit a lady I had been ministering to that was dying. Then many times He would tell me to pray for people dying when I was so desperate for prayer myself.

He taught me the beauty of aging people/elderly. The world looks at them like they're old and discarded. God doesn't. He looks at them like this is YEARS of battles on their faces. Years of struggles, prayers, tears, love, etc. There is nothing like an elderly woman crying to the Lord. Just beautiful!

He taught me what it is like when God takes His children to Heaven. It is the most BEAUTIFUL AND HOLY EXPERIENCE! His presence fills the room and he bears witness with the people present that HE WAS THERE! He gives the dying person peace during the transition. I will blog one day about what I saw with dying people.

He taught me how Satanic Hip/Hop music is - For over 10 years I coached cheerleading and hosted cheerleading competitions where I promoted little girls dancing to this terrible music that is doing nothing but leading them down the fleshly lustful trap. This music tries to define to our generation what a woman should LOOK LIKE and ACT LIKE! Terrible! I repented.

He taught me about the Gifts of the Spirit - Especially Discernment of Spirits. I was with one of my friends one day and I said something to her and in the spirit I saw a shadow fall on her of jealousy.

She didn't talk to me after that day. It greatly affected our relationship. I saw so many things...especially religious spirits and Jezebel spirits. He just opened my eyes to the spirit-realm.

He gave me new friends - As I released the old worldly friends, he blessed me with awesome pastors that can really impart into my life. He's given me all kinds of new Christian friends.

He taught me more about being a servant - He did this through the 101 year-old man I prayed for and God allowed me to enter Heaven with him and through the pastors in this city. It's funny now looking back because now I'm a servant to pastors/the bride. I learned in Bible College what it means to serve a pastor. So, here we go.

He taught me HOW TO LOVE others - People like real and authentic Christians. They want to know that you have been broken and have compassion. As God delivered me of my sins and transgressions and cleaned me out; he POURED more of himself in me. More came in and more went out!

I discovered my LOVE for SOULS - I never knew I was called to preach! God showed me that I am and when I'm loving/preaching...I feel like a vampire after blood, lol. It fills my heart with satisfaction when I can help and love others. It REALLY gives me blood back when someone gets saved. I crave soul-winning! If I haven't ministered in a while, the devil starts pointing out my surroundings (focus starts going to myself). As soon as I minister...I'm on fire again! LOL. It's my drug of choice.

I learned that even when people are in comas and dying, their spirits are still much alive and they hear you! When I went to pray for people that were dying, I would talk to them like they were sitting there looking at me. Their bodies are just shells and it may have failed them...but their spirit (the REAL person) is still alive and desperate for prayer...and maybe even salvation.

I learned that I'm nothing and HE IS EVERYTHING! It doesn't matter your smarts, wits, money, family, nothing....we are nothing compared to His Holiness! I need Him!

My love of gospel music/soul music. To me the gospel spiritual music is real. When African American people really sing under the anointing...IT IS POWERFUL! It also helped during my trial.

I learned not to question God on the prophetic! I learned not to question Him in how someone reacts to the Holy Ghost.

I learned that you are going to gain enemies and there is nothing you can do about it. Just give them to God. He knows.

I learned that he is my Soon Coming King; Lord of Lords, Died on the Cross for Me, and I'm his Bride which means when someone sees me...they see Him. I'm his Ambassador with ALL AUTHORITY, RIGHTS, HERITAGE, PROMISES, AND PRIVILEGES. I operate from the Kingdom of Heaven's Laws and Provisions.

I am to obey and serve Him in ALL things. This is where my victory and provision lies.

I cannot leave an assignment until God tells me to. I must stay where I'm planted until He tells me otherwise. This means that no matter how much I'm suffering or how much my flesh is crying out!

I learned that IT'S NOT ABOUT ME! Whenever I get to feeling that things are too stressful and my flesh is being rubbed too raw, I know it's time to fast. I must fast to put my temple in subjection and under God's will. Sometimes the 'ole flesh will rise up to me and say, "I'm tired of doing without money! I want a job and to be normal like everyone expects of me!" It's basically when I'm having a pity-party on myself when I have to fast. After a few days, my spirit man is back in control and that thing BREAKS off me.

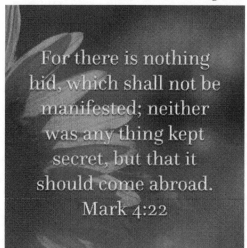

For there is nothing hid, which shall not be manifested; neither was any thing kept secret, but that it should come abroad. Mark 4:22

12
OBEDIENCE IS KEY TO YOUR WEALTH

When I was in Bible College, this came as a revelation to me based upon my answer to my daughter when God kept blessing us financially. She looked at me with tears on her face, "Mom, why is God doing all of this for us?" My answer, "Because obedience is the key to your wealth! I obeyed God and came up here and now He's rewarding us." This revelation is what I'm still standing on today.

Now, here's the deal; how do you define wealth? Well, it isn't all money.

Wealth can mean in your relationships as in a wealth of love from friends and family. It can mean a wealth of favor from God everywhere you go. It can mean a wealth of wisdom that just keeps being downloaded to you from Heaven. Wealth can mean so many different things versus money.

However, I also believe that God wants all His people to be prosperous. I'm not supporting the full prosperity gospel to where they invite you to their meetings and say, "I know 20 people here are going to give $10,000 each today and come up here and we will give you a personal prophecy." I don't believe in that. However, I do believe that God will prosper His children that are in full obedience to His perfect will.

Your Job is Not Your Provision

YOUR WEALTH IS IN OBEYING GOD!

One of the names of God is Jehovah Jireh – My Provider.

Let me clarify: Our job is not WHO WE ARE.

Our job is not our provider. It's an AVENUE that God may use to bless you.

We are who we are in Christ. We are hidden IN HIM. On your death bed people are not going to say, "She was a great lawyer." At that point, who cares? Rather, we want them to say, "Wow, she left a legacy and changed so many people through obeying God."

As far as providing...I know plenty of people who work and STILL don't have enough. They're living paycheck to paycheck. Not living their dream...not following God...just surviving! Who wants to live like that just because society says you should?

I also know of people who get any job that comes along, and then they are not able to go to church. You never see them again. They either work so much they're exhausted or working during church times and can't come to get refreshed. How is that of God? They may work all the time but money is still lacking.

The key is to have wealth by obeying God, no matter WHERE that may take you. He may give you a dream of an invention that will give you continual money flow. You never know. But we only LIMIT GOD...He is immeasurable....deep and wide!

Rather, live life to the FULLEST for God and let HIM lead you where to go. If He says...go to Bible College....then do it. If he says...start a food ministry with nothing...then DO IT. He may say to work somewhere. The point is to FOLLOW HIM. Your wealth is not the way society says it should come. You may acquire wealth...but NOTHING like the wealth the Lord will provide in His path.

IT'S IN OBEYING HIM. If you're obeying Him and he gives you a job...it's because there is people there He wants you to reach. IT'S ALL ABOUT SOULS. So, whether you're working by society's expectations or not, make your life count and just trust God. Just do what HE says to do because HE knows best.....not man. Most of our GREAT PREACHERS stepped out and trusted God. We don't have to UNDERSTAND why...we just do it.

When He opens the door it's WIDE! He shuts them and controls when to open them...especially when you are putting your 100% trust IN HIM.

Trust God and walk in HIS plan.

The Perfect Will Versus the Permissive Will

There is a big difference between perfect will versus permissive will. The perfect will is saying, "June, I want you all to myself because I'm a jealous God!" The permissive will I may turn around and do because I can't die to ALL that He's asking me to do is to still go to church all the time, serve my pastor to the fullest, and do everything else that is good in the world EXCEPT the ONE thing that God is asking me to do! That is the permissive will.

Another example – God tells Joe Blow to start preaching. Well, since he doesn't want to pay the full price to do God's perfect will, he starts a charity to help homeless people so that he can keep up his lifestyle that he wants. People in the community are praising him because he's doing such a noble thing. However, underneath the good actions, he's really in disobedience to God. So, God may have to allow things to happen to him because he is not obeying God.

FYI – when something happens to you whether in sickness or some type of tragedy, the first thing you should do is examine your heart. Go to God and say, "Lord, is there something I've done to cause this to happen? Have I opened the door to the enemy somehow?" So, we should always examine our hearts and make sure the door is shut to the enemy in our lives!

Once you know you're in 100% obedience to God's will, then just hang on for the ride and trust God.

13
JESUS IS THE TRUE HUSBAND

After my experience with trusting in Him 100%, I definitely consider Him the true husband. I know that when I get married again, how He defines His role in the relationship. I hope I can explain it well:

Jesus is the true husband. You lean on Him for all your needs even when you're married because your husband is only flesh. Whenever he messes up, it doesn't throw you off-track. You just simply go to your true husband and say, "Lord, your son made a mistake. He's your son before he's ever my husband. Please help your servant. I know you have a plan for him. Thank you Lord. I trust you as my husband. You're going to take care of me. I don't trust man, I trust you."

By us always keeping Jesus in His place it will make our marriages much better. We know who our hope lies in. We know that our marriage to this person is an assignment just like any other assignment. We can't leave until God releases us. According to His word, He hates divorce! So, we stick by that person until such point that God designates whether it's through death or He comes back after us. Yes, sometimes divorce is necessary, but it should be a last resort for sure.

Here's the deal about Him being the true husband:

He never leaves us

He's close to us at all times

He's very affectionate

He takes care of us

He supplies all of our needs

He always looks out for our best interest

He warns us to prepare us

He talks to us – it's always open communication

He always thinks positive of you

When He disciplines you it's for your own good

He is with you at all times

He thinks you're beautiful no matter how ugly the world thinks you are!

He knows what makes you smile

He likes to shower you with gifts and affection

He gives you the comforter to teach you and to hold you when you need it.

He gives you angels to look out for you at all times

He always knows what's ahead for you so He guides you

He intercedes to the Father on your behalf at all times

So, he's everything we ever need as a husband.

This is what He will not do:

Beat you.

Threaten you with harm.

Smack you around.

Put you down.

Hurt you.

Put more on you that He knows you can't handle

He doesn't talk about you to others and demean you or belittle you

Want you living in poverty

Tell you anything against God

How awesome is that to have a husband that is always looking out for your good? I've had husbands that are not like that. It's not fun to live like that.

Satan is a Legalist

Think of Satan like a policeman. He watches to see when we sin then it opens the door for him to move in. We must open that door first. A lot of sicknesses happen because of disobedience and sin. So, a Christian, whenever something happens to them whether it's sickness or anything bad, they should first ask God if they have opened the door to the enemy.

14
LIVING YOUR DESTINY AS HIS BRIDE

When a person says, "OK Lord, take my life and do with it what you want and I surrender ALL." You are basically saying, "I want to be your bride." Jesus takes that seriously and begins the process. Get ready because:

Bride, now he's courting you - When a man dates a woman he courts her. He wants you to know all about him. This is where I was raised. This is my family. This is my mom...my dad. My sisters, brother, etc. He begins to reveal to you who he REALLY IS. He wants you to know the things he's been through in his life. He wants you to experience HIM. How do you experience Jesus? SUFFERING! He begins to separate you and allows you to be abandoned, humiliated, shamed, etc., because he wants to know if you will accept his ULTIMATE GIFT....which is the dowry he paid for you...his life!

While you're suffering people turn away from you because they don't want to look at your pain. People like WINNERS...not losers. You look like a loser and weak to them. You are now experiencing life like Jesus did. People spit on him, shamed him, humiliated him, hit him, etc. He suffered! You will suffer!

So, after you suffer, repent, run through the fire, been under so much pressure sometimes you feel like you're going to explode, etc., then the devil comes to see you. When you get to the point that you say, "Father, why have you forsaken me?" The devil looks you square in the face and lies to you, "Stop the insanity, go back to the BOX that everyone thinks you should be in. Go back to the old familiar system that says, 'Work yourself to death. You have a master's degree, you should have a job! Something's wrong with you because you're not successful driving a new car, a new home, etc.' You don't want to go down that suffering road and marry Jesus. You don't even know where you're going. You will be rejected, persecuted, and no one will love you."

At that point the Christian makes a choice. We look that devil in the face and say, "Get thee behind me Satan! I know what I'm getting in to and I choose to marry Jesus no matter what I lose. I give myself away. My life is not my own. It's Jesus'."

It's like when Jesus said, "Father, forgive them for they know not what they do." He means all the people that he died for. So, we make that decision to keep going to the unknown and for real marry Jesus then. Once you get past the crossroad, then the wedding takes place.

The crossroads is this:

There are two systems on Earth.

• **The Kingdom of this World system** (Tree of Knowledge) that has Earthly laws and under the rule of Satan. The world tells people how they should "mold" into acceptance by doing certain things or following a certain pattern. (Everything makes this system too like music, movies, news; everything that floods your eye gate and ear gate).

• **The Kingdom of Heaven System**. (Tree of Life) This is the unknown. This is unfamiliar and polar-opposite the kingdom on Earth. This system tells you a different identity.

Now Jesus is ready to take you as His Bride because now you TRULY KNOW HIM AND KNOW WHAT YOU'RE GETTING IN TO! YOU know that you may lose your life because you are in a system that is of this world. You will then be a foreigner in a strange land. You are ready to take on the Kingdom of Heaven principals within this foreign planet. Think of it like Chronicles of Narnia. We are here with our fleshly bodies but we don't BELONG HERE. We walk in the spirit thus we are led by the spirit, but we live on Earth so we must obey Earthly laws as long as they don't penetrate the Heavenly laws. For instance, God says "Do not lie". So, no matter what...we DO NOT LIE.

So now you're ready to get married so the Lord prepares you like Esther to marry the King. He will prepare you and beautify you.

It's basically that you are taking on HIS Identity! You are now Mrs. Jesus Christ. When the world sees you...he sees HIM. You walk IN ALL AUTHORITY in Jesus' name! You have access to His inheritance.

When you get to the end of yourself and God has drained you of your past; then you meet the Lamb that was slain for you. It's a beautiful love story. Romeo and Juliet are now Jesus and you. This is how he means it to be. You die for each other.

When he puts that wedding band on you. It's gold (representing his heritage, inheritance, laws, etc.) and it's round (representing eternity, time never ends).

He puts that ring on your finger and SEALS YOUR LOVE THROUGHOUT ETERNITY! Greatest love story ever told!

As your husband, he is the gift giver. He showers you with gifts because He loves you and wants the world to know how much He loves you. He wants you to be proud and to brag about what he does for you. He showers you with gifts because he loves you. He wants the whole world to know how he treats you. He gave me a house, a car, and beautiful clothes.

He wants to be EVERYTHING to us! This is why I went through the trial! I have to KNOW HIM. I have to be able to tell women all over the United States that Jesus is my husband and my provider! He will give me a house, car, etc. He's going to take care of me!

But ye are a chosen generation, a royal priesthood, an holy nation, a peculiar people; that ye should shew forth the praises of him who hath called you out of darkness into his marvellous light:
1 Peter 2:9

P.S. After I left the throne room, I called some people that rejected me and told them I forgive them and wanted to be restored because I know now that God allowed them to do that because I had to identify with HIM. So...I'm so thankful for his mercy! :)

I'm excited about the future! I know that with a job, without a job, without a house, with a house, with no one or with everyone...I don't operate in this Kingdom...I know who holds my hand and about the ring of eternity on my finger and seal me! :)

Scriptures to Know Your Destiny

Matthew 5:11

1 Peter 5:10

1 Peter 3:14

1 Peter 4:16

1 Peter 2:20

Acts 5:41

Acts 9:16

Romans 8:17

Romans 8:36

2 Corinthians 1:7

2 Corinthians 11:23

Philippians 3:10

2 Timothy 2:12

Hebrews 11:25

James 5:10

15
PURITY & HOLINESS FOR HIM
INTIMACY WITH YOUR HUSBAND

Remember when God asked me to die to my life and how he wanted me all to himself and my argument was, "How can you have sex with me as a husband?", well let me reveal what He has shown me about intimacy with our creator.

First of all, sex was meant to be between a man and a woman to procreate the Earth in marriage. A marriage is a holy covenant between God and two people (trees) on Earth (His garden). When those people make the covenant, they become one flesh.

How can two literal people become one flesh? It's the same way as when we take communion and partake of His flesh through the bread. It is symbolic as I'm consuming your flesh in my spirit. We become one with each other because we then become one unit to God.

When a husband comes to God the Father and makes a petition to the throne, he is representing a household to God. Think about how God did in the Old Testament. When he saved one person, he saved the whole household. It's because in God's eyes they're all one. Also consider Adam when he saw Eve and he said, "You are bone of my bone and flesh of my flesh, thus shall we leave mother and father and become one."

Jesus wants to be one with us as husband/wife relationship. All of the Bride, whether man or woman, is His wife. He refers to the church as His Bride. Being one with us is expressing intimacy through communications and worship.

When you worship Him, you are giving Him the fullest expression of your body, heart, soul, and spirit. You are making Him the center of your attention. You are lavishing Him with love. This is why He loves it when we worship Him. It's just basically telling Him that He is that special to us that He has our undivided attention. We are expressing our love for him through dance, tears, raising hands, or other forms of worship.

For myself, I can't tell you the times I have felt His presence so deep on me that it is almost like ecstasy. It's the equivalent of it. I can almost feel Him, touch Him, etc.

When you have a relationship with God and you're intimate with Him, you can feel His presence. You have an awareness that He is with you at all times. He has angels with you to protect you. You are in a bubble. You are in a dome of protection. You are shielded from all danger. Once you backslide you feel that dome has been lifted and it's a scary feeling because you feel like you're thrown out there to the wolves. I've been there, done that, and bought the T-shirt. It's not a good place to be at all!

Many times when I worship He talks to me. Sometimes I go in the throne room. What I mean by that is I enter the secret place – the Holy of Holies. You know when you're in there because it's entering another realm. Sometimes I've stood before the throne. Literally, the throne. He's talked to me, loved on me, judged me, rebuked me; given me open visions, etc. It's amazing when you can experience your creator outside of this earthly realm.

Sometimes when I go to bed and I'm sad about something that happened during that day, I will say, "Lord, I need some lovin' tonight. I feel really sad." Then I will feel like a glove all over me. It's like a warm blanket. Sometimes when God gives me a dream, I will feel the Holy Spirit come over me before I go into it. That's the intimacy of God.

The Holy Spirit and Intimacy

When I read Benny Hinn's book, *Good Morning Holy Spirit*, it changed my life! I highly recommend it! To realize that the Holy Spirit is a real person and wants to have a relationship with you and that you can talk to him as a real guide on this Earth…that's pretty awesome! I began building a relationship with Him! I will talk to Him like, "Holy Spirit, what do you say about this?" "What do you want me to do?"

I tell children He's like a superpower! God gave Him to us to help us make it on this Earth. Also, now that I know about time and the destiny that God has for each person if they will just give it up to God…then I really know how valuable the Holy Spirit is!

If you do not know the Holy Spirit as your best friend and real guide, then repeat after me, "Holy Spirit, please reveal yourself to me so that I can live the life that you want me to live. I surrender all to you and allow you to take my body as a living sacrifice for your glory. Please help me Holy Spirit."

The Bible says if you seek Him you will find Him!

> Put on therefore, as the elect of God, holy and beloved, bowels of mercies, kindness, humbleness of mind, meekness, longsuffering; Forbearing one another, and forgiving one another, if any man have a quarrel against any: even as Christ forgave you, so also do ye. Colossians 3:12-13

Intimacy with God is also through prayer. When you pray in tongues and enter into that holy place, it's very intimate. It's just you and your loving God having a conversation. No one on Earth can understand what you're saying. It's a special language that God gives each person and that just shows how intimate He wants to be with us. What a loving God that He gave each person their own prayer language so that He could talk to them and through them on Earth. That is a powerful thought! Intimacy through prayer....there's nothing like it.

16
OUR RIGHTS AS HIS BRIDE - BRIDEFEST

Now, how does the Bride become acceptable to God to marry His son? This is a powerful question! The Bride must lay it all down and die for Him. She must totally surrender her/his tree to God. How do they lay their lives down? By living in 100% obedience to God.

I do a ceremony with We are the Bride Ministries called Bridefest. This is where the Bride has a prophetic wedding and she surrenders all to Jesus. This is the itinerary of the program and it will show you how God gave this ceremony to me in a dream. He gave me this dream when I married Him on October 27, 2013 in Clarksville, TN at God's Place Church. Pastor played the part of God and a church member played Jesus. My family came to watch and my brother gave me away. It was a special moment.

The Wedding Before Daddy God
(Bridefest Prophetic Wedding Ceremony)

Ceremony Begins with God and Jesus standing up front looking at Bride

God speaks:

My heart leaps for joy today because my purpose is fulfilled. I allowed you son to die for my creation. I allowed you to be the Lamb, sacrificed for the sins of my people. When you hung on the cross and suffered for my people, I found your life a happy exchange for my creation. Son, you CHOSE to stay on that cross for our creation.

When Satan approached me about these my children, he told me how they committed many vile sins. He fought to destroy them for many years. Son, I accept your sacrifice for my sons and daughters. I consider you worthy my son to marry my children.

Bride, I have examined your heart and found your repentance for your sins acceptable to my throne. I have tested you, tried you, and caused you to experience what my son experienced on the Earth. I am required to mold you into a beautiful piece of pottery for my glory to shine through you. In order for my glory to reside in your temple, I must clean out the baggage. You endured the trials and suffered much pain in this life.

I see you made the CHOICE to die for MY WILL to be completed in your temple. I accept your sacrifice sons and daughters and find you WORTHY to be Jesus' Bride. I will use your life for my glory and finish what I began in you.

There are two systems on Earth:

The Kingdom of this World - The Kingdom of this World is ran by Satan. Through this Kingdom he tries to lure all mankind to deception through music, television, media, society, and all Earthly things. He tries to convince people that His way is the acceptable and right way to live. He tries to convince mankind "Do What Thou Wilt"...be selfish, be a humanist, put YOURSELF first. It's all about you. He offers humans fame, fortune, pleasure, etc., like he did Jesus on the mountain.

The wages of sin is death. Pleasure is only temporary. Beauty is judged from the outside and is fake. It's a false identity. This kingdom shall pass away. It's all a lie and used to drag my children to Hell.

Kingdom of Heaven. - The Kingdom of Heaven is polar opposite. In this Kingdom, people put others first. We prefer others before ourselves. We love our enemies. We forgive and hold no ought. Beauty rests on the heart...on the inside of a person. Jesus is the King of this system. Jesus exalts those that humble themselves and obeys Him. In this Kingdom, you will be persecuted because as they hated me, they will hate you. You may have to die physically in this system. However, my rewards are GREAT! My ending is happiness and eternity with me and your loved ones.

To Both of you, your marriage is a binding contract to endure through the ages. Sons and daughters, your lives are SEALED in Christ as you accept the price you must pay to continue in the Kingdom of Heaven's path for your life. Your destiny is purposed for GREATNESS! No man has seen what I'm about to pour out in you. The Heavens have been opened for your life. You have been CHOSEN for SUCH A TIME AS THIS MY DAUGHTERS AND SONS!

Vows Between Jesus & The Bride

Jesus speaks:

Brides, by this ring I thee wed. The circle of the ring represents eternity. I seal you on my heart throughout eternity.

Your flesh shall NOT EVER SEPARATE MY LOVE for you. The diamond represents my promises for you:

As my wife you now have all rights to my inheritance, my promises, my rights, my dominion, MY NAME, and all authority of the Kingdom of Heaven.

As I place this ring on your finger, may you always know while you're living on Earth in your flesh, that I am ALWAYS with you.

I promise the following:

- To never abandon you!
- To never abuse you!
- To love you ALWAYS!
- To provide and take care of ALL OF YOUR NEEDS!
- To protect you!
- To always consider your heart and thoughts in our communications.
- To always listen to you when you want to talk.
- To provide your intimacy needs
- I will be your healer
- To hold you when you hurt
- To take care of your children! I will save your WHOLE HOUSEHOLD! Like I did Moses, Lot, etc.
- I will be your EVERYTHING!
- You will be my Queen and always be cherished!
- You will never lack again!
- I will never allow you to be put to shame!
- I will shower you with love, gifts, and affection.
- We will be together throughout all time and eternity!

Bride speaks:

Jesus, I'm so thankful I made the decision to fall into the waters of faith with you. I thank you for forgiving me of all my sins. I humble myself before you my Lord! Words cannot express my gratitude for you dying on the cross for my sins.

So, my Lord, my sovereign King, my Lord of all Lords, I CHOOSE to die for you too. I give you my ALL. My life, my children, my whole past and identity. I give you ALL of my hopes and dreams. I give you my flesh and if it may cost me in the future to die for your name, THEN SO BE IT!

I choose to serve you until DEATH BRINGS US TOGETHER.

So, with this understanding, I vow the following to you:

I give you my body as a living sacrifice. I will walk in Holiness Lord. I shall not defile my temple.

I will be pure and holy before your eyes. You have washed me clean. I am a virgin again before your eyes. You have made me pure and holy again. I shall not defile my temple again. You bought me with a price. YOUR LIFE was the ultimate price.

I will obey you with all of my heart!

Where you send me I will go!

What you tell me I will do!

I will obey you AT ALL COSTS!

I will serve you

I will keep a servant's heart and serve your people

I will defend the helpless, the fatherless, the needy, the hopeless, the children

I will preach and be your witness to the lost and gather souls for your Kingdom

I will please you all the days of my life

May my life be a Lifesong to you my King

I will take your Identity on myself

I will be honored and proud to represent you Lord

I shall NOT be ashamed!

Even if it requires my Life...

• Let YOUR WILL BE DONE LORD

• I will DIE for you!

So, with this ring, I thee wed.

I vow to secure my life and be hidden in you.

I vow to walk in ALL AUTHORITY of your Kindom and principals!

I vow to obey and serve you all the days of my fleshly, Earthly life

I vow to keep my flesh pure and holy and reserved until you allow me to marry an Earthly man

I will seek you with ALL MY HEART

I will seek your face in all of my decisions

I will respect you as the Head of my House!

God speaks:

Before you kiss the bride, I must confirm the meaning of this kiss. When Jesus kisses you Bride, it means he is GRANTING YOU his authority in our Kingdom…all rights! The mouth represents authority. Out of the mouth speaks life and death. From this point forward, be very careful with your words because you will be representing Jesus on this Earth. You will be Mrs. Jesus Christ.

This means when you go places, the demons will tremble because you are Jesus walking and taking dominion. Walk in your authority and rights. Change the world! I will work my will in your life! Don't look to the right or left, look to me for your help. Do not fear what man may think or say. What can man do to you?

Jesus, you may kiss your bride…

Jesus kisses the Bride

God speaks:

I now introduce, Mr. and Mrs. Jesus Christ! These are my Chosen Warriors on this Earth. My blessings are flowing over them life like a river now. NOW! Please welcome her Body of Christ!

The basic point is that the Bride lays down her life for Jesus as Jesus laid down His life for her. They marry each other and it's the perfect love story. It's better than Romeo and Juliet although this is a death on both sides…but to their own wills.

> *Ephesians 5:27 – That he might present it to himself a glorious church, not having spot, or wrinkle, or any such thing; but that it should be holy and without blemish.*

The Bridefest ceremony is a prophetic public ceremony deepening the commitment of the Bride towards our savior. We vow to lay down our lives for Jesus Christ. We strengthen our relationship with Him as we either freshly say our vows or renew our vows! It changes people's lives!

This is how we know our authority is by knowing who we are in Christ. Once we know our position, then we know our authority!

17
HE IS JEALOUS FOR THE BRIDE

The judgement that is coming to the Earth is because He is jealous over us. He is not going to allow His Bride to have another lover before Himself. Think about how He did with Israel. When they turned their backs on God He ended up having to whip them a little bit and turn them over to their enemies so they would realize how much they needed Him.

Well, it's the same with my life. It is a great example of how jealous He is. He would not quit until I just completely died to myself. He wanted every part of my being and it's that way for every person on Earth. Let me share this revelation He gave me:

What is an Idol?

As you all know now how codependent I was with men, think about all the other things I was doing. I smoked 3-4 packs of cigarettes a day. I absolutely loved them crazy things! I was addicted to sex! Whenever I was sad about something I'd always smoke a cigarette. Or, I could turn around and go have sex with someone. Or, I could go eat a big meal and make me feel better. Or, I could call someone and say, "Hey, let's go get a drink, I'm hurting and need to talk."

Well, the Lord revealed to me that "Anything we put before God when we are hurting is an idol to me." So, if I'm hurting and I reach for a cigarette, alcohol, sex, food, conversation with humans, etc., that is an idol. God wants to be our all-in-all. He wants to be the leaning-post in our life. If He thinks you put something before Him, he may take it from you or cause you to have something happen to cause you to repent to put Him in His proper place.

Well think about America right now. Our country has gotten so off-course from our relationship with God, it's just sad. We are a Christian nation and will be that way as long as Christians are still in America. We only surrender it if our wills give up. The only reason God hasn't wiped this country off the face of the Earth due to abortions right now is because of the praying Christians we have. Think about the entire remnant that is here in this country crying out to God!

So, because of our smacking God in the face so many times by taking Him out of schools, the public sector and now mocking Him by our Supreme Court granting marriage rights to homosexuals, it is forcing God's hand. He is going to have to whip us a little bit and turn us over to our tormentors for a while so that we will repent and come back to Him.

Now, here's the deal….the remnant will be protected. I was in an intercessory prayer group one day and had an open vision. I drew the picture and this is what was on the picture:

I saw Obama on the gold Olympic stand. He was on the top and to the right at the bottom on the silver stand was an eagle. To the left was a bear on the bronze stand. Out of Obama's mouth was a double-edged sword to each one. Behind him were all kinds of natural disasters. I drew bombs, a tsunami wave, earthquake, tornado, etc.

It represented chaos behind him. Then underneath the Olympic stand was a dome. Underneath the dome was plush green grass. Inside the grass were shiny gold crosses. Over Obama was another dome. Inside this dome was plush green grass and Israel.

So the group I was with said that it meant that while chaos was going on in the world that the Christians and Israel (Jews) would be protected in the dome and be prospering. It would be an outward appearance of God's blessings while the Earth was collapsing.

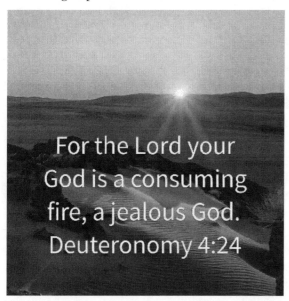

For the Lord your God is a consuming fire, a jealous God. Deuteronomy 4:24

Well, I believe this to be true. The coming persecution on the church will be both a blessing and a curse. Curse because many will die and lose their life. Curse because families will be torn apart, etc. Blessing because we will not suffer the wrath like the sinners.

Blessing because we will not starve when others will. Blessing because we will be prosperous.

So, the point is not to be shaken when things fall apart, lean on God so that He can show you things to come.

He doesn't want you to have an idol and lean on it versus leaning on Him. He loves you.

God shall likewise destroy thee for ever, he shall take thee away, and pluck thee out of thy dwelling place, and root thee out of the land of the living. Selah.
Psalms 52:5

For there is nothing hid, which shall not be manifested; neither was any thing kept secret, but that it should come abroad.
Mark 4:22

18
PRAYER FOR YOU AS HIS BRIDE

I pray this book has blessed you and caused a hunger to rise up within your spirit to want to draw closer to God. I pray you make the decision to lay it all down and to surrender all to the 100% perfect will of God. How do you know the perfect will? You get before Him and let Him show you.

Seek ye first the Kingdom of God and all these things will be added unto you.

We have come to a place in time that we can no longer just play around with Christianity. It may cost you your life now. We m u s t rise up to the destiny that God has called us to whether it means death to the flesh or death to our will and desires. We must follow Him at all costs.

I want to pray with you so that your life can be prepared to endure during the final days on Earth. God had you read this book for a reason and it's to lavish His love on you today! Just repeat after me:

Dear God,
I surrender all. Please forgive me for any acts of disobedience I've done in my past (name them if you know them). Help me Holy Spirit to walk according to your destiny book that you wrote for me before time began. I want to live the fullest life that you have designed for me. I cancel any negative word that's been spoken against my destiny or my life! I renounce any allegiance to Satan I've made in my life. I renounce any acts that I've done willingly or unknowingly that made a pact with the enemy. I refuse to live a mediocre life. I want to follow you to the ends of the Earth in full obedience to your will. Thank you for making my crooked paths straight. I plead the blood of Jesus over my eyes, (eye gate), my ears (ear gate), my mouth (mouth gate), and over my heart. I pray you cover me in your wings and place me underneath that dome of protection. Please heal my roots of any bitterness from over the years. I forgive everyone that has ever hurt me (name them if you need to) and ask you to forgive me for hurting others. I release all hindrances of my past to you Lord. I release my past, my failures, my sadness, and my hopes and dreams to you. Thank you Lord for writing a new chapter in my life and I give you the pen to my book. In Jesus' name. Amen

ABOUT THE
AUTHOR

Dr. June Dawn Knight resides in Clarksville, TN and is the President of We are the Bride Ministries based in Nashville, TN. She is also the President of Visions Communications and Treehouse Publishers. She is the mother of three children and three grandsons.

She received her Doctorate in Theology at the International Miracle Institute in Pensacola, Florida in 2015 under the direction of Dr. Christian Harfouche. She received her Master's Degree in Corporate Communications from Austin Peay State University in Clarksville, TN in 2012. She received her Bachelor's Degree in Public Relations in 2011 from Austin Peay State University. She previously attended World Harvest Bible College in Columbus Ohio, which is now called Valor Christian College under the direction of Dr. Rod Parsley. For more information go to www.junedawn.com or www.wearethebride.us.

Made in the USA
San Bernardino, CA
26 June 2020